Lead Us Not Into Trent Station

Memories from Long Eaton and beyond

Richard Guise

Published by Richard Guise

Publiohed by.
Richard Guise
E-mail: richard_guise@yahoo.com
Mobile: 0788 443 2011

Printed by:
Mastaprint Plus Limited
1 Bradley Street
Sandiacre
Nottingham NG10 5AH
Phone: 0115 939 1772

ISBN: 0 9545587 0 7

Front cover:
- Split-windscreen Morris Minor and author at family picnic, circa 1957. *Photo: author*
- OK, not Trent Station actually, but a northbound departure from Quorn & Woodhouse on the Great Central Railway, 1980s. *Photo: author*

Back cover:
- Sutty the Corolla in the South of France, 1990. *Photo: author*
- Tiananmen Square, Beijing, 1993. *Photo: author*

Lead Us Not Into Trent Station

Acknowledgments

My thanks are due to all the characters that appear in this book. They're all real, but – with a few exceptions – I've spared their blushes and my legal expenses by changing the names.

Thanks to Jim Faulkner, Carole Shaw and Craig Bee for reviewing drafts of this book. Any remaining errors are clearly my fault.

RGG
July 2003

1

The Three Squares

The world I first knew was small and orderly, and so was I.

Every morning at eight o'clock the Co-op milk float hummed its way around The Three Squares, replacing our white plastic tokens with pints of milk, followed at half past ten by the Co-op bread van, replacing the blue ones with loaves.

Monday was wash day, when mimam[1] let me turn the mangle while she fed the sheets out of the dolly tub. Tuesday was a day for best behaviour and for being very, very careful eating crumbly scones off flowery plates at Nana's; it was the jam that caused the trouble. Wednesday was rent day, when Mr Windlass parked his beige Standard Vanguard right outside our entry. He could have parked it anywhere on Albert Road, because the only other cars in the street – Mr Craddock's grey Wolseley, Mr Marriot's black hearse and midad's light blue Morris Minor (FDB 932) – were all out at work. FDB 932 was parked in the yard of Clumber Street Co-op, where midad was the manager. He met mimam when she used to work upstairs in the cash office at 'The Central'. I'm pretty sure everyone in town worked for the Long Eaton Co-operative Society in one way or another.

Thursday was fun, because Thursday was half-day in Long Eaton, when midad came home early to take us all a ride in the car, to the 'beach' at Ratcliffe-on-Soar or to the 'mountains' at Charnwood Forest. Friday was bath night, which meant shivering in front of the dining-room fire before crinkling up my eyes in the soapy water of the little green bath. (Don't get the wrong idea: there was a proper

---

[1] I could write 'my mam' and 'my dad', but you'd be saying it wrong in your head, at least wrong for Long Eaton.

7

grown-up bath upstairs as well.) Saturday was market day, which, if it was Long Eaton, meant a glimpse of Mr Handlebar, or if it was Nottingham, meant the smell of fish and pomegranates. And Sunday was, well, the day when time stood still.

On a map, The Three Squares looked like three slices of toast set out beside the Market Place. The streets between the slices were Albert Road, Broad Street, Laurence Street, Alexandra Road, Edward Road and Milner Road. Most of the ten years I lived there I couldn't say 'Milner', and so I called it *Minler* Road. To make me feel better about this impediment, mimam, midad and misister also called it Minler Road. My Uncle Harold said he thought it really *was* Minler Road, but then Uncle Harold said a lot of things that weren't really true.

Nothing much happened in the Three Squares. Correction: nothing *at all* happened in The Three Squares. Even though the Russians were launching Sputniks (I loved that word), and people were shooting at each other in Suez (wherever that was), Long Eaton seemed to be in a different universe where things just never happened. Though these uneventful days must still have been a precious relief to mams and dads, signalling an absence of blackouts, rations and explosions, such thoughts were beyond the ken of the small boys in our gang, the Albert Road Club. Well, if nothing was going to happen, we'd have to make it happen. And so, with our native English resourcefulness, the five of us set about inventing, designing and building a fully operational, 60-foot submarine.

No, just kidding. We played street games, like everyone else. When mimam got fed up of my plaintive "Mam, I 'an't goranythin' to dooo!", she'd despatch me round to Alan Waites's. Alan Waites was my best friend and lived three doors away. His house was on the corner of one of the squares and so it had a bigger garden than mine. He had two trees – one of them you could see from my garden – some bushes you could get behind, and a wall without windows that you could kick a ball against. Alan probably didn't live there on his own, he probably had some parents or something, but I never saw them.

If we saw any of the gang in the street, the chances are we'd play Braer Bear on Edward Road. (Maybe Braer isn't spelt like that, but street games aren't for spelling anyway.) The rules of Braer Bear are simple. The one who's 'on' goes up Edward Road and hides somewhere – somewhere being up an entry or, in summer, behind a bush. Then the others – who've been standing on Albert Road outside No. 28 with their eyes closed, counting to a hundred – turn the corner to start their perilous progress up Edward Road. Their mission is to get to Milner Road without being 'dobbed'. The mission of Braer Bear, the one who's 'on', is to dob them, with the words "Dob! You're on!". Pretty groundbreaking stuff, I can tell you.

Many years later, some foreigners – from London or Yorkshire or somewhere – claimed that we lads of the Three Squares did not invent this tense and skilful game, and – an even greater absurdity – that it was called Tag. I will admit that Braer Bear was a variation on Dobby, which everyone in Long Eaton played. What was unique about Braer Bear was that it had to take place on Edward Road. If you played it on Milner Road, for example, it wouldn't be Braer Bear, it'd be merely Dobby. Obviously. And in any case, you'd be mad to play it on Milner Road, as there were no entries to hide in on the factory side, and we weren't allowed to go on the canal bank, so you'd be getting dobbed all the time. No, I've no idea why it was called Braer Bear.

So this was my world. The universe beyond started at the red phone box on Broad Street, where you could turn right past the library to Sawley, then Castle Donington, then Birmingham, then London, then the English Channel, then New York[2], then the Wild West, then the Moon, and then Outer Space. Every time we drove past that phone box I'd check for my holster and space suit. I still do.

Moccasins and Handlebars

I knew a lot about the Wild West, and not just because, like my Three Squares pals with tellies, I was completely goggled by the box. You couldn't drag me away from *Rawhide* ("Gid 'em urp, roooll 'em out!"), *Bronco* ("Bronco, Bronco, tearin' across the Texas Plain", *The Cisco Kid* (I'd have given all my pocket money for that hat), *Tenderfoot* (why did he change his name to Sugarfoot? – I still want to know) or especially from the bestest of the best – *The Lone Ranger*.

---

[2] Europe didn't exist in the '50s.

9

Apart from having the best signature tune (Dangdadalang... etc), the best mask, the best horse and the best Injun (Tonto), *The Lone Ranger* had the unbeatable feature of also appearing on the big screen: for 6d every other Saturday morning at The Palace. You've seen those clips of young lads in short trousers riding their trusty steeds in the padded seats at the pictures – well, that was me and those were my trousers. It was over thirty years before I discovered that 'tonto' is Spanish for stupid, and that Tonto's gruff riposte to the masked white man – "OK, quenosabe" – means, more or less, "OK, he who knows nothing".

My other, private source of Wild Western knowledge was Uncle Harold. Like two others of midad's family, UH had emigrated from Long Eaton to America. Unlike the others, he kept coming back. And, more's the point, coming back with Indian moccasins and menus from the Queen Elizabeth and stickers from a BOAC Comet and pennants from the Boston Red Sox and pictures of big red cars and sparkling skyscrapers and tales and tales and tales. UH had built this house, he'd bought this car, he'd crossed the whole of America in it – the *Whole* of *America!* – he'd got lost in the Mojave Desert, seen rattlesnakes, heard coyote. Coyote! Even saying the word lifted me straight out of Long Eaton and dumped me into a tumbleweed gulch with the Lone Ranger, Tonto, Silver and Scout. There wuz Injuns out there an' we'd have ta sit under the desert stars all night, listenin' out fer the crack of a dry branch over the squeakin' o' them darn crickets and the howlin' of the ol' coyote. God, I sat at UH's knee and hung on every word. Skyscrapers 'n' cowboys, Red Sox 'n' Injuns – nobody told me they were a hundred years apart – they were all in the same time and place to me: right now and right over there. All Long Eaton had to offer was Mr Handlebar.

Oh yes, I'd seen a few famous people all right. You had to if you wanted to hold your head up in the Albert Road Club. I'd seen the Mayor of Long Eaton, I'd seen the Bishop of Derby, I'd seen the Queen (well, actually just the Queen's train; well, actually just the bridge that the Queen's train had passed over a few minutes before) and I'd seen the greatest of these by a mile: Mr Handlebar. Every Friday or Saturday, when mimam took me to Long Eaton market[3], there he'd be on his stall by Deacon's Bank, standing on a wooden beer crate, waving articles around for admiration by the ladies in

---

[3] When it was in the Market Place, where markets should be.

scarves (I never noticed what the articles were), shouting in a strange accent and sporting an enormous, I mean absolutely *gi*normous, handlebar moustache. And – get this – his name was Handlebar too! It was, because I read it printed in big letters above his stall. It *was*.

Out and About

I liked going out anywhere: three doors away to Alan Waites's, two streets away to the pictures, three streets to the market, down Tamworth Road to mimam's friend Mrs Banks's (play table skittles), a bus to Auntie Polly's (play the harmonium), a walk to Nana's. Actually no, let's not get carried away here – I did *not* particularly like going to my Nana and Granddad's (mimam's parents), because 1) they didn't have anything for me to play with, 2) I had to have my hair combed *very hard* before I went and 3) mimam told me *very* sternly that I must be on Best Behaviour, which I knew translated to "Don't fiddle with the doilies, for goodness sake don't break anything and you *must* eat everything you're given – yes, even the crusts!" Yuk.

Nana and Granddad's house on Douglas Road was bigger than ours, had a front garden as well as a back one and in those days was near a five-bar gate onto the fields where Petersham Estate now sprawls. None of this made any difference to the simple fact that it was b-o-r-i-n-g boring. Now, if they'd told me that Granddad's brother had been a comedian, joined The London Musical Company and in 1911 gone off with them to China, Hong Kong, Malaya and India, where he'd bought a coconut grove before dying of smallpox in 1915 and being buried in Calcutta, I'd have paid attention. He had, but they didn't, and so I didn't. Instead, I just stared out of the window at the smoke drifting up from the chimneys opposite, wondering if they'd make good cover from Injuns' arrows.

"Rick, eat up your cucumber or you'll be early to bed!" Even today, whenever I see a serviette or a flowery plate, a cake stand or a doily, I need to get out fast.

It was a bit better down Recreation Street, where some aunts and uncles (midad's family) lived. They had a piano, a seat that opened up, trains at the bottom of the garden and, down 'The Drift' at the end of the street, a big oak tree and some allotments where I could get dirty helping midad dig up the potatoes. And where I could also break my arm by jumping two inches from a railway fence onto a tuft

11

of grass. Darned rough country, Derbyshire. (In fact I specialized in Dumb Ways to Break a Limb: another one was tripping over a Yorkshire terrier while playing Braer Bear and an even dumber one was several years later.)

Most of the trains that chuffed southwards past The Drift were on their way to what was undoubtedly the most exotic location within the bounds of Long Eaton: Trent Station.

Before Mr Beeching[4] had two of them demolished, the town had three railway stations: Long Eaton, Sawley Junction (now Long Eaton) and Trent. Of these, Trent was the only 'proper' station, i.e. with an island platform, a forest of semaphore signals, a herd of porters and a station buffet. To access the island, if you arrived by car, you had to park in a little lay-by on Trent Lane and then descend on foot through a low-roofed, echoing tunnel before you emerged via a wide flight of stone steps with maroon railings into a happy hubbub of trolleys, whistles and steam. Even more thrilling than this, however, was the pedestrian route from 'Monkey Park'[5] along The Pad, which was squeezed between the mainline and one of the town's many ballast holes (now Forbes' Hole), and finally across a series of wooden sleepers that led you, probably with your labelled, dark-brown suitcases, across the actual railway.

From Trent, steam trains squealed, rattled and puffed in all directions, to such fantastic destinations as Sheffield (where Michael Palin was probably waiting in equal wonder at the time), Leeds, Carlisle, Glasgow and of course London St Pancras. Trent Station was famous for confusing unwary passengers who'd alighted just to change trains, by having two trains going to the same destination, but departing in opposite directions – such was the complexity of curves around this former hub of Midland Railway operations. I wish I could go and sit there now, just for one evening of unalloyed excitement. Quite why, every Sunday morning, we had to implore The Lord Himself to "lead us not into Trent Station" I never

---

[4] His report was published at noon on Wednesday 27th March, 1963, but I later discovered that Beeching was not the villain he's generally held to be, since he was simply asked how British Railways could save money. Destroying half the network was of course a valid answer. The guilt lies with the government who couldn't see beyond the end of their car-obsessed noses. Indeed, some of them still can't.

[5] Now the roundabout outside The Tapper's Harker.

understood – God evidently wasn't a train-spotter and it was probably this sorry failing on His part that first made me suspicious of Him.

Alas, Trent Station no longer exists, but – unlike God – it really did exist at one time, and I was there. And you know what? I've a little inkling that, some time in the 21st century it's going to exist again. There, Mr Beeching, put that in your stack pipe and smoke it!

The other exotic escape available within Long Eaton was its cinemas, but these, alas, have fared even worse than its railway stations, for, of the three cinemas on offer in the '50s and '60s, not one remains. My first picture was *The Great Locomotive Chase* at The Empire, whose ornate façade stood where subsequently Tesco and now W H Smith occupy one of the ugliest buildings on the Earth's surface. What sticks out in my memories of The Scala, which does still stand – just! – is queuing as far as the Derby bus stop for Cliff Richard's *Summer Holiday* (I admit it!). Long Eaton's last cinema to survive was The Screen, which was previously The Ritz but which, when I regularly queued up there with those three threepenny bits (inflation) gripped in my sweaty little palm, was The Palace. Here, after the days of the sixpenny *Lone Ranger*, came such sources of teenage wonder as *Swiss Family Robinson, The Great Escape, You Only Live Twice* and *Every Home Should Have One*. Every *town* should have one and it's a sad indictment of local planning that endless supermarkets now cover whole swathes of Long Eaton, while no-one can conjure up a single cinema screen.

Getting back to the plot, though, it was because of the Midland Railway rather than The Palace that Long Eaton is my home town. Granddad Guise had moved to Long Eaton to work at Toton Sidings. I just about remember him: he had a big sharp nose, steely eyes and hard hands that ruffled my hair. Wherever he went, I used to walk around so close to his feet that mimam worried he'd tread on me, but he never did. I don't remember Grandma Guise, but everybody else in the family says they can remember her coming to the rescue when mimam and dad didn't know what to do about a single hair, sharp as a knitting needle, that was sticking out of my head when I was born. It made me look like a baby unicorn. After a lot of umming, aahing and general dithering by everyone else, my Grandma pushed them aside and, with a single stroke, yanked it straight out. I yelled and yelled, but, although I still can't remember you, Grandma, let me take this opportunity to say "Thank you". Nobody would have given me a job with a horn sticking out of my hat.

My Granddad had moved from Droitwich, Worcestershire. When I was little, one or two of the old folks still lived there and once every few weeks we'd pile into FDB 932 on Sunday morning and turn right at the red phone box to head for Birmingham and beyond. Aunt Lou's house was dark and frightening, and so was she – I think even her doilies were black. But the journey there and back gave me a chance for some back-seat driving with my blue plastic steering wheel, complete with gear lever and horn – "Stop pressing that now, Rick, or I'll take that map off you!". The road map was the other good thing about a day in Droitwich.

I think I knew my NSEW before my ABC. There were always maps and atlases in the house. Midad said he read maps in the war. (I mean, I'm sure he did, but I suspected he did some other stuff too,) Going down to Droitwich, I followed every inch of the route, looking up in the yellow *AA Handbook* every Breedon-on-the-Hill and Ashby-de-la-Zouch, quizzing the rest of the car on their county, population, miles from Nottingham and best hotels – information I hoped I kight need one day. Keeping my finger on the map, I'd poke my head up at the window – or out, if allowed – to scour the road ahead for yellow AA motorcyclists to be saluted or white road signs to be devoured. 110 miles to London down there – I think I saw Picadilly Circus! 75 miles to Holyhead up there – in another country, on an island – hey, I heard a seagull! I *did*!!

The other great map-reading events were holidays. These consisted of a fortnight in August, at first always Skeggy, but then some pretty exotic places: Bournemouth, Bispham, Scarborough, Holland-on-Sea. Yep, I was a pretty well-travelled fellow. En route to Skegness, when I could lift my nose from the map, I'd always look out for the sign to New York (2 miles), and then try my best to be the first to spot Boston Stump, then the Water Tower, then the Clock Tower and then, then – yes, there it is – that streak of grey between the grey mud and the grey sky – the Sea!

We always stayed at the Saxby Guest House, just off Drummond Road. It was OK. It had breakfasts. But, to be honest, I can't remember anything *inside* at Skeggy – *outside* was the place for me. The warm sand in my toes, the cold sand on my buried chest, the thwack of plastic cricket bat on rubber ball, the puff-and-hiss of the rubber ring, the rattle of the miniature train at the back of Unity (our chalet), the two-stroke-diesel smell at the boating lake (it's still there, smell an' all), the frantic tapping of the Crazy Golf tournament, the oink, click and whirr of the Waites photographers on South Parade, the delicious pink stickiness of the candy floss at the fun fair, the bracing sea-spray of the beach ferry, the rustle in the trees along Coronation Walk after midad had bought the News Chronicle from the shop with the green verandah. Great times. Simple times, you might say, but they were great to me.

The Afternoon that Time Forgot

Holidays loom disproportionately large in my memory, for you tend to remember what comes down the years in photographs. But since midad only got the two weeks' holiday a year, I must have spent years and years and years in the Three Squares. Most of that time seems to have been Sundays.

As any child – or at least any child astro-physicist – will tell you, time is warped on Sundays so that, at the limit, the day never actually ends. Hence the film *Forever Sunday*, starring Cliff Michelmore and Jean Metcalf. All right, I just made that up.

Here is the schedule for 532 of my 567 Sundays from 1951 to 1962:

- 8:30 a.m. Get up, eat sausage, clean teeth, get dressed, let mimam brush my hair 57 times, get told off for not cleaning teeth properly, clean teeth again, stand still to have hair brushed 23 more times.

- 10:15 a.m. Go to church, say hello to 43 grown-ups, listen to 43 grown-ups admire my shiny hair, kneel down, stand up, listen to 43 grown-ups sing The World's Most Boring Songs, sit down, listen for approximately 12 hours to Father Bannister warning us about the dangers of Trent Station, stand up, listen to Even Boringer Songs, kneel down, mumble something meaningless, stand up, get patted on the head by 21 old women, go home.

- 12:15 p.m. Listen to *Two-Way Family Favourites*, with Cliff Michelmore in London, Jean Metcalf in somewhere called BFPO (light crackle) and Wally Wonker in Australia (heavy crackle) talking about barbecues (whatever they are); cringe as midad sings along with *The Folks Who Live on the Hill*, eat roast beef and Yorkshire Pud (not bad) and apple pie (pretty good), listen to *The Navy Lark* (excellent – "Left hand down a bit.").

- 2:15 p.m. Start of the period when Time Stands Still. Watch midad having forty winks, listen to mimam knitting, listen to clock ticking. "I 'an't gorranything to do!" "Just sit quietly, our Rick. It's Sunday afternoon." I know it is – time's standing still.

- 2:16 p.m. Three hours have passed. Practise gunslinger's reverse draw.

- 2:17 p.m. Grow eyebrows[6].

- Sometime the following century. Listen to *The Brains Trust*. An old man seems to be talking about 'flossafee', which must be a kind of candy floss I've never had.

- 5 p.m. Have tea: tinned peaches (not bad) and fairy cakes (pretty good). Dry up. Carefully. "Yes, I'm *being* careful, mam. I *am*."

- 6 p.m. Be swayed back into that Sunday stupour by the syrupy strains of *Sing Something Simple* ("Doo-di-doo-di-doo-di... sing something simple for youuuu annnnnd meee... This has been Sing Something Simple...") You're telling me it has. Ask if I can go to bed. Ask again.

---

[6] Something I was later to regret.

- 8 p.m. Try to sleep till Monday.

I have a theory, called **The Theory of Adulthood**, which states:

The week you grow up is the one when you stop dreading Sunday afternoon, because there's nothing to do, and start looking forward to it, for the same reason.

According to this theory, I grew up in a Welsh seaside resort one week in October 1970.

Back in the '50s, though, I'm pretty sure my Sunday afternoons were a staple childhood experience. All children have their escape routes from boredom and to my four – playing street games, dreaming about the Wild West, going places and reading maps – was soon added a new one: a fad that started in the 1950s and, well, turned out not to be just a fad after all, since some people are still at it over 40 years on. Do I mean hula-hoops? Give me a break! I'm talking of course about pop music.

The Red Box and Further Miracles

Elvis had been there in the background for a while, on *Family Favourites*, in *The Radio Times*, at the pictures, but frankly – and I know this heresy will make you put this book down and throw it straight into the Caribbean[7] – well, frankly, Elvis seemed just a bit sissy to me and my pals. I mean all that "Uhu uhu", all those Hawaiian shirts, all that dancing, all those girls! Yuk. No, what made my nine-year-old ears prick up when it came crackling out of our Bush wireless was the country twang of Johnny Duncan and the Blue Grass Boys ("Last Traiiiin to San Fernando"), the strangled vowels of Adam Faith ("Wish you wurnted mah lurv, *boy*bay") and especially the doing-badoing of the Shadows... preferably without that nit Cliff Richard. More heresy. I went to see *Summer Holiday* for The Shads, you understand.

Then, one glorious day in 1960, midad came home with a red box that, in one single revolution of its rubber-matted turntable, despatched Braer Bear and The Lone Ranger to the old tumbleweed of history: our brand new Dansette record player!

Yes, it belonged to all of us, and yes, we had to agree between us on our first two singles, but that didn't stop me stroking its mottled red

---

[7] That *is* where you're reading this, isn't it?

17

lid, clicking open its little golden latches, carefully lifting its beige metal arm and blowing the dust from its tiny but precious stylus as though it were my personal pet. Recently my nose passed close by a box made from the same material as those Dansettes and immediately the untrammelled joy of those early disc-laden days washed over me once again.

For the record (ouch), our first singles were Elvis's *It's Now or Never* (accepted under duress) and The Drifters' *Save the Last Dance for Me* (I hope, I think, I'm sure this was my choice). Even now the Drifters' first "You can dayans…" makes my toes tingle and drops me straight back in that Albert Road dining room with feet twirling around on the maroon carpet to the magic sound of the Dansette, which took pride of place on the shiny dining table – protected by a couple of doilies, of course.

My sister and I played those two singles to death. More had to come, or else mimam and dad would soon be going bonkers. My sister bought more Elvis while I bought the Shadows' *Apache* in its kaleidoscopic Columbia sleeve. That one got played so much it got warped and it still is, because – like all my singles except one[8], I've still got it.

As anyone from Britain around the same age will surely recall, singles used to cost 6/8, EPs 13/4 and LPs around 32/11. So my 5s-a-week pocket money meant a fortnightly visit to Gilbert's, which used to be a fab electrical shop on Long Eaton High Street, since demolished to give access to a ghastly new market. As electrical appliance stores sold record players, they also sold records, and so, like thousands of others across the country in the '50s and '60s – including a certain North End Music Stores in Liverpool managed by Brian Epstein – Gilbert's was transformed on Saturdays by a swarming mass of youngsters bustling past the Hotpoints and Frigidaires to the record department at the back, where they'd flick eagerly through the racks, check the B sides, peer at the new charts on the wall – the printed national NME chart or the coloured, home-made pegboard for the store's own chart – and pass a suitably disapproving comment to their mates that Helen Shapiro was *still* Number 1. I generally knew exactly what I wanted, but that didn't

---

[8] And if whoever borrowed my *Penny Lane / Stawberry Fields Forever* (picture sleeve) is reading this, you can still leave it quietly on my back doorstep and no action will be taken.

stop me flicking and peering, as well standing on tip-toe in the listening booths to get an earful of the latest releases – in fact the previous day's releases, as records always came out on a Friday. What I wanted more than most in those days was 'The Big O' – Roy Orbison.

The Shads were OK, Del Shannon was pretty cool, but when push came to shove – or rather when 6/8 came into my hand and the man had a new single out – it was Orbison for me. First, what a great name – sounded a bit like 'orbit', a bit outer-space. Second, all that warbling and wailing – what a performer! Third, those shades – not many photos of pop singers beyond Elvis and Cliff filtered through to the Three Squares, but when I saw Orbison, he looked just so, well, mysterious. And finally, let's face it, the man was no Clint Eastwood, but a rather overweight and chinless chap who consequently had none of those silly frizz-haired girls drooling over him. This was my man!

As if it wasn't enough being able to play the Big O's records at will, a further miracle happened when news filtered through to the Three Squares that he was not only in England but soon to appear at the Nottingham Odeon! I can't remember what pleas or negotiations took place, but the long and short of it was that I was going to be there. It's all a bit of a blur – I don't even know who went with me – but there I was at the back of a low and smoky hall, while in the distance, between the swaying heads was the real, living, warbling Orbison. This knocked Mr Handlebar into a cocked hat. Even the other acts – Freddie and the Dreamers and Brian Poole and the Tremeloes – seemed small beer next the Main Man. Even writing this now, I'm not sure it wasn't just a small boy's daydream.

Strangely, the Big O was not universally adored by my school chums. I remember a Saturday morning that must have been in 1964, when four of us sprawled head to head on the carpet with Ian Hopkins' Dansette. Ian was also an Orbison devotee, but Roger Martin and David Mills favoured a new and breezy Californian combo called The Beach Boys, and offered vocal accompaniment to a newly acquired copy of *I Get Around* ("yeh, get around ooh-oo I get around") as proof. Ian and I made our point by wailing the backing vocals to the Orbison classic *Blue Angel*:

Orbison: "Oh, Blue Angel"

Hopkins and Guise: "Wow wow wow"

19

Orbison: "Don't you cry"

Hopkins and Guise: "Wow wow wow wow"

Orbison: "Just because I"

Hopkins and Guise: "Wow wow wow wow"

Orbison: "Said goodbye, oh, wow"

Orbison, Hopkins and Guise: "Wow wow wow, ooh oh wowow wowooh!"

Yes, you're right – it could be that Roger and David's predilection for The Beach Boys heralded a step in the right direction for western popular music.

A bit battle-scarred they may be, but my Big O singles are all still there in their blue-and-white-striped London American sleeves: *Only the Lonely, Runnin' Scared, Cryin'* etc etc – classics to a disc. When, thirty or more years later, The Big O finally went to the big recording studio in the sky, it was like losing a big brother. On the annivresary of his death, I shared another spontaneous duet version of *Blue Angel*, this time without the benefit of the actual disc to help us, with a tall Dane called Lars in a French cafeteria. Our wow-wow-wows were doubtless even worse than in that Sawley semi 25 years before, but at least this time we got a round of applause from the table of bemused French engineers.

Back in early Orbison days, even my devotion to pop music as such wasn't shared by the old Albert Road Club. They were more interested in Ford Zephyrs, BSAs and the Archers (the local speedway team, not the radio programme). So we sort of drifted apart. While they were still outside on the Three Squares in search of chrome wings and knobbly tyres, I'd already shifted inside, with my ear glued to the whirr of the Dansette and the crackle of Radio Luxembourg. And it wasn't just the arrival of the red box that ruptured the old routine, but also one of the three events that, for me, signalled the end of the '50s and the start of the '60s.

1. Long Eaton Market Place when it was actually a market place. Although this view was taken in 1973, several classic 1960s cars appear. The main Nottingham-to-Birmingham road, the A453, passed plum through the middle of Long Eaton until the Clifton-Kegworth link road was built. *Photo: author*

2. The Co-op seemed to run just about everything that was anything in Long Eaton. This is a 1973 view of the 'Café' shop on Station Street, so called because of the catering facilities elsewhere in the building. This 'Central' grocery later moved across the road, then into the 'Co-operative House' department store and then to its current location opposite High Street. *Photo: author*

3.   A million miles from Long Eaton! Photos from relatives in America, like this 1966 scene, were like glimpses of another planet – possibly the planet Orbison. Is that *six* cars in the drive?! *Photo: author*

23

4. A goods train rattles along the Toton High Level line past Recreation Street one winter's day in the 1950's.
Photo: author

24

5. I lived for our trips out. This family picnic, circa 1957, could have been almost anywhere in the sunlit fields of Derbyshire, Leicestershire or Notts. Split-screen Morris Minor FDB 932 was our means of escape from Long Eaton. *Photo: author*

2

The Irksome Four

Historians are keen to point at events that mark the end of an era: the assassination of Archduke Franz-Ferdinand, the fall of the Berlin Wall etc. But we each live through our own eras and, unless you're Frau Ferdinand or your address is 1, The Wall, Berlin, they don't correspond to these global events, do they? For me, the 1950s ended twice: on 14th December 1961 and then again on 17th September 1962. The '60s finally started on 3rd September 1963.

One day in early Autumn 1961, as we all sat down to tea at the kitchen table, midad announced – as coolly as if he were reading the weather forecast – that we were going to move house. My sister and I were silent for two seconds and then the questions came tumbling out over the jam sandwiches.

"Where to?"

"When?"

"Has it got a big garden?"

"Has it got a bomb shelter?"

"Will I have my own room?"

Mimam didn't ask any questions, so I think she must have known already. As the answers came, I knew this was going to be the most exciting thing in my nine-and-a-half-year life. Even more exciting than going up in a plane at Ingoldmells. (The excitement of the live Big O was as yet unknown.) We were going to move across town to a detached house that midad had bought. Detached! Bought! It had a big garden with four sheds, a greenhouse and a fish pond. A fish pond! There were apple trees, pear trees, raspberry bushes and gooseberry bushes. Midad didn't know exactly how many trees.

There were so many trees he didn't know how many – wait till I tell Alan Waites that!

"Mam, can Alan Waites come round and play in our garden?"

Mimam hadn't been paying much attention. "What? Oh well, he might want to come round for tea one day, if his mam will let him."

If you didn't count the railway embankment at the bottom, the new garden was a quarter of an acre. ("Dad, can we call the 'ouse *Quarterofanacre?*") It was in a cul-de-sac, three houses from the dead end. ("Can we call it *Dead End?*") At one end of the street was the speedway stadium and a chip shop; at the other end – our end – was The Drift, for it was in fact Recreation Street, where midad and his eight brothers and sisters had been born – even Uncle Harold – and some of them still lived there.

So we moved, on Thursday 14th December 1961, the year I could write the date upside down in my jotter[9], and for me the 1950s had ended. Since this move from one side of Long Eaton to the other, I've moved more than a dozen times myself. Whatever promises I make to myself about throwing things out, each time I move there's more accumulated rubbish to move than there was before. In 1961, at the age of ten, I put all my things in a Co-op biscuit box. I don't know how all the rest of our stuff moved. All I know was that one night we were on Albert Road and the next on Recreation Street.

I remember the smell of gas when we moved in and I think midad probably took care of it. I remember the new goldfish, called Fred and Sam, being introduced to the pond: "Fred, this is the pond". I remember watching the trains go past and counting the coal wagons (top score: 63). And then one afternoon I remember mimam died.

The 1950s had ended again. From the vantage point of thirty, forty, fifty years on, such events are as prominent as a windmill on a fen, but to a ten-year-old they take a while to sink in. That teatime I knew this was something big, but, when all said and done, it *was* teatime and teatime meant *Popeye* at 5 o'clock. I watched it at my aunt's that day and Popeye the Sailor Man seemed especially reassuring.

There were some changes of routine, though. One of my aunts didn't work and so she usually came down the street to give me and my

---

[9] Next occurrence, trainspotters: the year 6009.

sister our dinner[10]. I didn't much like Auntie Nora's hot jam tarts, with the burnt paper still stuck to them. When she wasn't looking I'd cut slices off and put them on the chair under the table. Ten minutes later, the slices would be cool enough to put in my pocket, so I could throw them in the Station Road litter bin on my way back to school. After a week of Auntie Nora's tarts, I'm afraid my grey shorts would be a bit on the sticky side.

Grammar Grubs

However, while the routine at home was upset for a while, school was as solid as a rock.

In England in the 1950s and 60s, the education watershed was at age 11. Before 11, you didn't know you were getting one. You led a generally carefree existence, while picking up a few essential skills, like how to multiply by twelve, how to spell rhythm, how to dribble a football past Glyn Sanderton and how to make a teacher look at everyone but you. If you went to Brooklands Junior School, you also got to see *The Dambusters* after school on Mr Reynolds' rickety old 16mm projector, which instilled the crucial idea that, being British, you could beat the world at anything by sheer application of your Britishness, with no need to resort to any actual violence – except of course for drowning a few Germans who jolly well deserved it anyway. You also got to go and look at some foreigners in the flesh on a school trip to Belgium, where you were quite amazed to see that, even though they did indeed speak utter nonsense and eat quite disgusting food, they moved around, drove cars, went shopping and generally behaved in every way as though they were actually human.

Then, at 11, you took your first ever examination, in which you multiplied by twelve and spelt rhythm, and the result of which set the tone for the rest of your life, by despatching you either to Long Eaton Grammar School, where you became a Grammar Grub, or to Wilsthorpe Secondary Modern School, where you became a Wilsthorpe Worm. While the Worms learned woodwork, the Grubs learned German. Apparently there was as yet no call for German-speaking carpenters. On Monday 2nd September 1963, I became a

---

[10] Note for southerners and foreigners: dinner in Long Eaton is what you have in the middle of the day. The one later on is called tea. 'Lunch' is something you have between meals, at around 11 a.m. and 3 p.m. Clear as mud?

29

Grammar Grub: the 1960s had eventually begun and suddenly I knew I was getting an education.

Before I share with you some of the irksomeness of life at Long Eaton Grammar School (or LEGS as we inmates called it), I will freely admit that there must have been *something* right about it, since, armed with the million facts and rules I memorized in my six-year incarceration, I've more or less coasted through the succeeding 30+ years, more or less in good health, more or less in the black, and more or less in full employment. I can't say that I've used every fact that I picked up – I can't, for example, recall the Battle of Crécy cropping up just yet, despite Miss Cantor having spent three whole lessons drumming its every stratagem into our vacant brain cells. But if ever it's needed, I know it's there.

The first thing I learnt at LEGS was that school was not a few huts and a field like at Brooklands, but a two-storey building with stairs, corridors, halls, balconies and a hundred rooms. Then I found out that teachers were not people like mimam, midad and Mr Reynolds, but monsters in black gowns for whom you had to stand to silent attention as they entered the room. Then, even worse, I found out that pupils were not your friends, but big youths in long trousers who gave you Flying Lessons.

Twice I've joined an organization that glories in an unannounced and unofficial initiation ceremony. They were both schools of some sort, which probably says something significant about education (but I don't know what it is). If you tried to implement an initiation ceremony in an office job, they'd fire you on the spot and you'd deserve it. The Flying Lessons at LEGS involved being bodily thrown from the top of a flight of steps into a small, prickly and well-battered bush. I thought I was going to die, but all I got were a few grazes that I had to explain away to midad. Within a week at LEGS, I'd learnt both to fly and to lie.

The girls at LEGS were an entire race apart. Even those who six weeks before had been my friends at Brooklands had suddenly gone alien. They had a separate entrance off the main road, a separate playground, and a separate flight of steps up to a separate door. I don't know whether they had separate Female Flying Lessons, since we boys were banned from their playground lest we molest them, or possibly they us. In fact, I don't recall ever speaking to a girl in my entire six years at LEGS – which, since they were actually in the same classroom, may seem a tad extreme. I must explain…

The Geography of The Classroom

Carter, Flynn, Guise, Haigh, Hall, Hickling, Higgins, Marshall, Miller, Patching, Plackett, Shenton, Start, Stevenson. Sitting in alphabetical order was just a part of the ethos of order which infused all aspects of daily life at LEGS. We 14 boys[11] of 1A sat alphabetically on the right in every classroom and in every subject, while the 18 girls[12] sat alphabetically on the left. This inviolate rule was theoretically waived in the sixth form, but was voluntarily continued even there, so well had it been embedded in our skulls. Later, when I attended my first university lectures, I naturally veered to the right-hand side of the lecture hall and was rather unnerved when some brazen woman would just wander in and sit in front of me – or even, heaven forbid, beside me! But these debaucherous events were still far off. At LEGS, decorum was strictly maintained.

Teachers addressed boys by their surnames and girls by their first names. Boys addressed each other by their surnames and of course avoided addressing the girls altogether. If put in an impossible situation, when "'er" was too ambiguous, we might mumble the girl's surname. But any boy caught using a girl's first name ("It worn't me, sir, it wor Deborah what started it") would suffer for it for at least the next four years: "Oooh, *Deb*orah is it?! When are you two getting married?"

Every classroom had five rows of desks, the outer two rows being single desks and the others double. Being early in the alphabet put me at a single desk near the wall, which kept me well out of the direct line of fire of most teachers. It also kept me as far as possible from the girls and next to a cupboard of books, through which I could browse instead of having to talk to people. The alphabet also put one Hayes by a blank wall. On this wall one day Hayes scrawled in a tiny biro script the word "ECCLES", which, as any true Englishman of a

---

[11] These are the real names and, apart from the occasional end-of-season promotion or relegation, remained so through 2A, 3A and 4A too. I've not used real names when writing about individuals.

[12] Apart from ending in Zimand, the girls' names mostly escape me now and so the least offence is caused by making no attempts to recall them here.

31

certain age knows, is not only a Lancashire town and a sugary cake, but also the most easily mimicked Goon[13]: "Oyoyoyoyo ... moy noym's Eccles!" Being sublimely stupid, Eccles was a great hero to 1A and therefore I assume Hayes' graffito was intended as neither gazetteer reference nor confectionery order. The teacher took the same view and despatched Hayes to the headmaster, who caned him. Hayes was instantly and eternally marked out as a rebel. Reputations were made swiftly at LEGS and made in granite. Hayes was relegated at the end of the first year, and therefore dropped out of the fast stream and didn't go on to do A-Levels. I wonder what he's doing now. He may be perfectly happy and successful, but I've always had the nagging notion that the Eccles incident determined his future and that this future was somehow 'worse' than it might have been. I've never seen Hayes since school, have no evidence for this ridiculous idea, and my whole attitude reeks of elitist snobbery at its worst. This too is what Grammar School does to you.

The only occasion on which the barriers between the sexes were officially breached was...

The Dancing Lesson

"Now pay attention, boys!" Mad Ron Barnett, our sportsmaster, strode around the changing room in his loud purple tracksuit. "Stop messing about, Hopkins. Now, next Wednesday, there's no need to bring your PE kit to school. Instead of Games, you'll be having dancing lessons."

To a boy, we all froze. Hopkins left off his attempt to hide Martin's muddy shorts behind the radiator.

"Yes, you heard right: I said DANCING. As in 1-2-3, 1-2-3. Marriot, if you leave your jaw like that you'll catch a hundred flies!" With thirteen pairs of eyes fixed on him, the sunburnt sportsmaster came to a halt by my peg and stood, hands on purple hips, track shoes wide apart.

"In next week's Games period, Mrs Barnett and I are going to drum some basic dance steps into all you oiks – *and* the first-form girls, God help them ..." He paused for breath before delivering the final blow. "... And then, on the evening of December 15th – yes,

---

[13] For the *really* uninformed, the Goons were the successors to the Bumblies and the predecessors of Monty Python.

Hopkins, I said evening – AFTER SCHOOL – you'll all be ready to skip the light fantastic at the first-form Christmas Dance."

Christmas Dance? With girls?! Our scrawny, half-dressed bodies, already fagged out by the rigours of a cross-country run, shrank even further. Thirteen willies trembled in unison. Thirteen imaginations foresaw the horrors of this latest nightmare of life at LEGS.

Hopkins broke the silence with a question: "Sir, can we do the Twist, sir?" A snigger passed around the changing room.

"This will be real dancing, Hopkins, not your Chubby Checker nonsense. Now, finish getting changed, boys, and I'll be back in five minutes – anyone still here gets 20 press-ups."

With that, Mad Ron left. As we pulled off the rest of our togs, Simpkins lightened the atmosphere a little with an energetic interpretation of the recent No. 1, "Let's Twist Again Like We Did Last Summer." Marriot and Hayes accompanied him on rhythm and bass tennis racquet respectively, while Hopkins beat the bongos, in the form of a basketball between his knees. I laughed from the corner but didn't join in. Pulling on my grey flannel shorts, I counted the days. December 15th. 12 days to D-Day. D for Dance. Just when I could glimpse the Christmas holidays on the horizon, another dark mountain had loomed up from nowhere to block the way. Maybe on December 14th I could ask my Dad to make some trifle, then I'd stick my fingers down my throat and be off sick. Anything but dance with the six-foot Deborah Kirkbride or, even worse – and I trembled at the prospect – with the Two-Ton Tess of 1A, Rosie Ranshaw.

The Wednesday of the dancing lesson dawned grim and cold. At quarter to two in the afternoon, a damp chill still clung to the school hall, as fifty first-form boys trooped in and glued their bottoms to the row of benches along the right-hand wall. Fifty first-form girls glued theirs to the benches opposite. We glared at each other across the brown gulf of polished Parquet tiles that lay between. Not even the shared fear of a torment to come could bridge the chasm between the sexes at LEGS.

33

Mad Ron and Even Madder Ronette[14] Barnett strode into the Parquet Gulf. This rare sight of the two sports teachers together was a bad omen. They were clearly going to 'do something' together. And after some embarrassing banter, indeed they did. Mad Ron placed a large 78 on the Dansette that sat on the edge of the stage, and a ghastly crackling filled the silent hall. He took Mrs B by the waist and, as a sickening swirl of strings gave them their cue, the disgustingly dapper duo proceeded to move around the Parquet Gulf in what can only be described as a Waltz. It could only be thus described because, along with the 49 other boys, I knew the name of no other dance, except the Turkey and the Twist. The Turkey and the Twist had one unbeatable advantage over the Waltz: neither required any physical contact with other members of the human race... least of all female members. We'd been wondering if we might get away with something like this, or even with one of those prissy folk dances where you just held hands (bad enough) and didn't have to face each other. But no, our worst fears had come true. It was to be the grip-em-and-whirl-em-squeeze-em-and-twirl-em Waltz. Yuk and double yuk.

As Mantovani crackled to a halt, the Bs, who were both purpally attired as usual, turned to face each other and, like a pair of Sumo wrestlers, deeply bowed. Their audience remained deeply unimpressed. Undeterred, Mr B advanced to the blackboard and proceeded to chalk out the basic steps in the same way that he had chalked out the details of rugby union's offside rules the week before. How attractive suddenly appeared the prospect of an afternoon in the cold autumn mud of the rugby field! Who on earth had dreamt up this torture? I suspected OMG[15] had put the Bs up to it. The filthy swine. Our dear headmaster had about as much idea of what eleven-year-olds enjoyed as a baked bean had of a Sputnik's propulsion system. I decided to devote a happy half-hour in bed that night to thinking up twenty ways of killing OMG. Torturing him and then killing him. I could stretch him over his big oak desk and then cane him to death. Maybe when he was half-dead, I'd place a blackboard by his ear and scrape my fingernails down it. I would

---

[14] Ron's missus was actually called Carol, but, in deference to Phil Spector's missus and the Motown sound which washed across LEGS a year or two later, we subsequently renamed her Ronette.)

[15] Old Man Grimes, the head of LEGS, as it were.

then slice his ear.... As I gaily considered these pleasant possibilities, I heard from Mad Ron's lips the dreaded words: "All right then, boys. Take your partners!"

Oh God, this was it. I T spells it. A few of the boys shuffled to their feet, and then, realizing their exposure, immediately re-stuck their bottoms to the bench.

"Come on, boys, don't be shy – the girls won't bite you!" Some girls in my class had the audacity to giggle at this. The swines! (The sows!, I mean.) At least they could sit there and be passive. *We* ere expected to actually *do* something. If anything was worse than having to touch a girl, it was having to choose which one to touch. The fifty boys dragged themselves from the safety of the benches and proceeded to cross the Parquet Gulf with all the speed and direction of a nervous platoon crossing an abandoned minefield.

Random as our progress was, the demon dice brought Hopkins and me to within a few yards of Kirkbride and Big Ranshaw. I thought of praying to God for a miracle – for a bomb to devastate the entire school perhaps – when a brainwave came to me from nowhere. Well, maybe it came from God. After all, God was a man and no doubt detested the prospect of having to partner the Virgin Mary at Heaven's Christmas Dance. That halo the Virgin wore looked pretty sharp and if He got too close it could easily damage His Holy Beard. From wheresoever it came, I hissed the gist of my brainwave to my fellow victim: "Oy, 'Oppy. Worrif we both ask 'em at the same time? Then thi' wun't know 'oo wuz asking 'oo. Thi'd jus' gerrup and choose wun each."

"Yerron", accorded my comrade.

We shuffled up and, in unison, mumbled our tempting offer: "Jowtow wanna dance laak?" How could they refuse? Before I knew what was happening, my sweaty hand was towing the massive and entirely silent form named Ranshaw to the middle of the Gulf, and The Mad One had once again set the crackling Dansette into motion. Mantovani lurched into his threatening intro and our deranged leader called on his troops fearlessly to place their right arm around the waist of the enemy. Carefully avoiding the enemy's eyes and keeping her at as great a distance as my short arms allowed, I did as was bid. Like every girl at LEGS from October to May, Big Ranshaw was wearing a nicely washed dark green woolly cardigan, and immediately my sweaty right palm began to create matted patches on it.

As Mad Ron barked out his instructions, all one hundred young heads turned rigidly to the floor, there to observe the gangling progress of the feet which so recently had seemed to be under our control but which now followed their own agenda. 1-2-3, 1-2-3, right-left-together, left-right-together... As if I wasn't having enough trouble, Ranshaw was supposed to be translating each instruction into its opposite – a task that proved mentally and physically impossible. As an extra job for us boys, Mad Ron ordered us to look up occasionally and steer. This led only to my catching Hopkins' eye as he endeavoured to see beyond DK's much taller shoulders. Seeing me, he lost all control and the two of them, who had been veering towards the wall for some time, clattered first into the bench and then to the ground.

This was too much for Mad Ron. He barked at Mrs B, who brought Mantovani's strings to an abrupt halt. As one, we all extricated ourselves from our mutual grasps and stared at Hopkins and Kirkbride, who were by now both bright red, but at least once again on their feet.

"All right, I can see we've all got a long way to go before any of you grace the Pally di Dance. Now let's try something else..."

And so the afternoon dragged on through one disaster after another. The music changed, the steps changed, the partners changed, but it was all equally ghastly. With ten minutes to go to the final whistle, Mad Ron tried to summon up some belated enthusiasm.

"OK, let's just try the Waltz one more time." (Groans all round.) "But this time, something a little different. Imagine that the two lines Mrs Barnett is chalking across the middle of the floor are the banks of a river, and when each couple arrives at the line, the boy will naturally lift up his partner, carry her across the river, and then start dancing again on the other side."

I saw nothing 'natural' in that. We looked at each other aghast... I noticed the girls were even aghaster than the boys. Ron had definitely flipped this time. My only consolation was that my current partner was Penny Morris, one of the smaller girls, and so I might stand a chance.

"Now, boys, find the partners you had the first time we tried the Waltz." Oh no... Ranshaw! Barnett, you 24-carat swine! Casting a baleful glance back at Little Miss Morris, I trundled through the confusion of bodies until I found The Big R. I noticed she hadn't been making any effort to find me and, being no Charles Atlas, I didn't blame her. I managed to position us just past the Chalk River, the further to delay the dread moment.

"All right", boomed Ron, "now this time the movement around the hall will be *anti*-clockwise. Music please, Mrs Barnett!"

Even now, forty years later, I would readily shoot Mad Ron Barnett on sight. As soon as Mantovani struck up, I gave my partner a single glance of panic and then bent down to put my left hand behind the Ranshavian knees. As I pushed, Ranshaw bent and I managed to raise the dead weight off the ground. Unfortunately, the sudden pressure of Ranshaw's free-falling torso was too much for my right hand and, head first, my partner hit the banks of the Chalk River. My hand trapped beneath her, I rapidly followed. As we pulled our battered selves to our feet, I heard Ron gaily calling out: "Never mind, Guise, you'll just have to swim across! Ha ha! One-two-three, one-two-three..." Strangely enough, the little river incident seemed to render insignificant the old foot-coordination problem and Ranshaw and I waltzed with a grim and deadly rhythm towards the next crossing, where sheer grit this time saw us safely over to the other side. As Mantovani heaved his final swirling bow, a hundred battered bodies heaved a communal sigh of relief. In a moment of exhilaration at the final escape from our torture, I even bowed to Rosie and she made a faint curtsy in return.

Was this the start of a teenage romance? Certainly not. Having failed to tell midad of the school dance, and trusting that there'd be no headcount on the night, I made no appearance at the main event. I don't know whether Rosie Ranshaw turned up or not, as I subsequently avoided the subject at all costs. And also managed to avoid every occasion that might involve physical-contact dancing for the next 37 years.

Swot

The only good thing you could say about the dancing lesson was that it didn't generate any homework, which was undoubtedly the most irksome of the many irks at LEGS.

We'd never had any homework at Brooklands, and it came as a bit of a shock. I never came out of this shock during my six years at LEGS and, out of solme reactionary sense of fear, always did my homework on time. I never heard of anyone caned for not doing their homework, but being singled out by the teacher at the next lesson and having your mumbled excuse cynically rejected was deterrent enough for me. With my head always in a book, from my position by the cupboard, and with my on-time homework, I was naturally branded a swot. I therefore became a swot. I therefore passed all my exams that mattered (except one – see later). I therefore, after briefly dropping out, went to university. I therefore boarded the Gravy Train, if not for life then at least for long enough to give me the confidence to assume I'd get any job I applied for. If there'd been any male Arnotts or Blenkinsops in the class, I would have sat at a different desk and might have been the rebel Eccles scrawler. Alphabet rules OK.

Bored by the Bard

The central teaching objective at LEGS was:

> Pupils must at all times and in all circumstances be discouraged from ever wanting to go anywhere near any subject studied here ever again. (If necessary, bargepoles will be provided.)

Well, most of the mixed bunch of teachers we endured from '63 to '69 undoubtedly did their utmost to achieve this. One exception, though, must have been Mr Baslow, our English teacher, since here I am writing in the language he taught us and placing colons where he taught us to place them: right here. Hang on a minute, though, didn't Mr Baslow achieve half his objective by putting us off English *literature* for life?

It's a bizarre concept if you think about it. When you've passed your driving test, you don't get extra lessons on *where* to drive, do you? So, having learnt *how* to read, why on earth did they think we needed to be told *what* to read? Anyway, ever since mimam taught me to read when I was about three, I'd read lots of stuff of my own choosing, mostly under the bedclothes by the light of my trusty Ever-Ready: epic adventures such as *Five Go to Mystery Moor, The Nottingham Forest Yearbook 1959* and *Barrington's Centuries, Ball-by-Ball.* True to the LEGS objective, though, Mr Baslow managed to dig up the most boring books you could imagine. He found *Jane Eyre,* a book so dull the only thing I remember about it was that it was green; he found a mind-numbing and event-free tale about a bunch of ecclesastical nobodies called *The Warden* (by the suitably named Trollope); and he found the one English author whose tedious scribblings are guaranteed to induce a deep coma in any sentient being: William 'Wherefore art my spelling checker?' Shakespeare. Why QE1 bothered sending English troops around the world I don't know, when she could have saved money by just despatching old Shaky to bore the natives into submission with his hundred thousand alases and alacks. As far as I'm concerned, the old man's only achievement was to prove that not quite all the bulbous-trousered half-wits of the sixteenth century lived in Spain.

Thirty years later I met a fellow disparager of the Bard – in fact the world's only Flamenco guitarist and Stoke City supporter – and we raised a glass or two of Rioja to our sound judgement. The footballing musician, though, also ventured to disparage Pink Floyd, proving that nobody's taste is perfect.

The Bum From U.N.C.L.E.

What about Maths, though? Surely here was something actually useful. Well, I was surprised that there was (were?) still some Maths left to learn. I'd done *sums* at Brooklands – and once you can add, take away, times and divide, what else could there be left to learn? The answer, according to Miss Bottom, was something called trigonometry.

OK, hands up those of you who sniggered when you just read the name of our Maths teacher[16] – and you are probably a balding, bewhiskered and upstanding citizen (even some of you chaps) – so just imagine the impact on a bunch of short-trousered eleven-year-olds. Now, to the credit of us lads in 1A, we pretty soon got over her name: we could eventually say it without sniggering, I should say by about 1987. She knew she was called Ma Bum[17] and may as well have changed her name to make it official.

So Ma Bum taught us trigonometry, which as far as I could gather, was a thousand and one ways to measure a triangle. Now, strangely enough, although my sums have come in pretty useful over

---

[16] And this was her *real* name, not one I've substituted.

[17] Note for American readers: this is bum, not as tramp, but as ass, not as donkey. Clear?

subsequent years – confusing the check-out brigade by giving them the right money before they ask for it, for instance – I can't recall ever, in the real world, being called upon to measure a triangle. I admit that some shapes do crop up from time to time: working out whether a rectangular balcony is big enough to have breakfast or checking if a cylindrical beer glass does indeed contain a pint – but somehow those triangles have just failed to show up. Which is a shame really, because Ma Bum seemed to be quite transfixed by them.

I have a theory, a sort of **Law of Laws**, which states:

> *The amount of time spent on a topic by a science teacher is directly proportional to how many laws there are about it.*

Not how useful or even how interesting it is, but just whether it appealed to some bearded old Greek two thousand years ago. I offer right-angled triangles as proof. This bias is rather a pity, because, if they'd have told us more about the things *without* known laws – for instance, the direction in which a fart cloud drifts, or the distribution of drawn games in the Football League – then some bright spark in 1A might have seen the light and offered them the law. And today's eleven-year-olds might be learning Hopkins' Law of Fart Dispersal. That would certainly have been a greater contribution to the classroom environment than Pythagoras and his damned triangles.

Ma Bum also came up with something called algebra. Now, to start with this sounded like it was going to be more useful, since she said it would tell us how to "discover the unknown". What a concept! First she named the unknown; she called it x. Good start, Ma Bum – straight out of *The Man From U.N.C.L.E.* Then she called two other things y and z. This is where my grasp of algebra began to slip. I never did quite get what y and z were. One thing did become pretty clear though: you had to know what y and z were in order to discover the unknown. In fact, it turned out you had to know *everything except* x in order to discover x. What a fiddle! If you're smart enough to know everything else, you probably know x too. What I needed was something where you started knowing *nothing* and it told you *everything!* Whatever algebra was (and I never did quite latch on), it was not this.

So much for Maths. I gave it up as soon as I could. Ten years later, and still in search of the unknown, I drifted into a voluntary Maths course at university, wondering if these scientific types had made any

40

progress, what with Man landing on the Moon and everything. And what do you know? Just like Ma Bum, this professor was still waffling on about ys and zs; only this time he'd got plenty of ds too, and even d-by-ys and, for all I knew, DIYs. Leave it out, prof – come back when you know the answers, not just the questions.

Scruff 'n' Fish

The actual science we did at LEGS was even more of a mystery. Our Physics teacher was Scruff, or Mr Futcher to his face, who'd just come out of university – which in 1963 meant he wore a baggy sweater, suede shoes and scruffy hair. If there'd been any music scene in Long Eaton, Scruff would have fitted in perfectly as the lead singer of The Oiks, but, unfortunately for 1A, there wasn't and Scruff seemed dedicated to science. In particular he seemed dedicated to pulleys.

Now, those of you who are concentrating on this otherwise incoherent ramble, may have spotted a pattern here. Every teacher at LEGS seemed to have a pet topic, and that pet topic always turned out to be so obscure as to have little chance of cropping up in the day-to-day life of a late-twentieth-century human being. With Miss Cantor, it was the Battle of Crécy; with Ma Bum, those infernal triangles; and with Scruff it was pulleys. He had little blue and red pulleys scattered around his lab like so many games in an amusement arcade. He even had a pulley to lift his board rubber off the floor and probably thought this was neat, and I'm afraid to say that half the class did too. With his shock of ginger hair, his groovy shoes and his toy pulleys, Scruff was something of a hero to this half. Being among the other half was my loss, however, because, when Scruff got on to something actually useful, like electric circuits or water heaters, I wish now that I'd paid attention. I wish so because in the intervening decades my homes have run on these kinds of things and when they go wrong I have to pay good money for someone to come and fix them – someone who paid attention to a Scruff-equivalent at school. Strangely enough, I've never yet had to call in the local pulley-repair man.

At Chemistry I was even worse. Our teacher was Mr 'Fish' Monger, who actually wrote in one of my school reports – and I quote – "Guise really hasn't got a clue." How right Fish was. Even today, when anyone starts talking about hydrogen atoms or the ozone layer, my mind goes numb, my eyes glaze over and I think I'm going to faint. I get the same reaction standing in the Etruscan room at the British Museum or when accidentally switching to basketball on TV. I think the medical term is Hysterical Disinterest. In the case of Chemistry, I also blame Snikpoh and the Boggle Sinks.

Snikpoh and the Boggle Sinks

OK, I know you think this is just an excuse for another inane subtitle, but I swear I'm telling the truth and, if Snikpoh were around today, he would back me up. Snikpoh was my best friend through the most irksome days at LEGS. To the teachers he was Hopkins, but when the craze for backward names petered out, two survived in general usage: Snikpoh and Esiug (yours truly).

Crazes were a constant hazard at LEGS. If you weren't up with the latest craze, you were out. B-O-R-I-N-G out. Sometimes the national crazes seeped through – I think my hula-hoop is still hooping around somewhere – but mostly they were home-grown. One day, a bunch of us were playing shove-ha'penny on the desks, when someone had the bright idea of using our 12-inch wooden rulers to propel the halfpennies around, which made a lot more noise, caused a lot more chaos and was therefore a much better game. We dubbed it 'thwack-ha'penny', before someone else found out that if you used a flexible *plastic* ruler, you could actually thwack a halfpenny from one desk to another. Now this was not only noisy but also had the advantage of being quite lethal, especially when you could afford to use pennies instead of halfpennies. I should point out to any younger readers that we are talking real old copper pennies here, not the namby-pamby little metric variety. Clearly, with a few pounds of base metal flying around the room, boggle (for that was what we called the lethal version of the game) was several notches more exciting than shove-ha'penny and thus spread around the third form like wild fire.

Yes, by now we were 3A, causers of general havoc to the gentry, and proud of it. When some idiot from 3C managed to get his head in the way of a boggling copper, the game was officially banned by the headmaster. What really annoyed those of us who'd been in at the start of the boggle craze was not so much the ban, which was if anything overdue, but the fact that the head's statement didn't even quote the official name of the game, referring instead to "a dangerous form of shove-ha'penny". This was typical of the school's attitude towards creativity, as we'll see later in the Art and Music lessons.

So what's all this got to do with my incompetence at Chemistry? Well, the Chemistry lab had long benches and sinks, and before the demise of the boggle craze, Snikpoh and I found this to be the best boggle pitch in the entire school. You could actually thwack your copper from one end of the bench to the other, in front of the very noses of Martin and Mills, and, if you got it just right, it would end with a tremendous clatter in the sink at the other end. By general agreement, this achievement was worth six points on the boggleboard. For some reason, Fish was not an aficionado of this game of skill and courage, a shortcoming he revealed by actually banning Snikpoh and me from his lessons.

Now, I'm fairly sure this was illegal, but neither Snikpoh nor I enjoyed the services of a lawyer, and so we never found out. In any case, it was a real skive, whose only snag was that we weren't allowed off the school premises, and so, for the duration of every Chemistry lesson, we had to wander around the school corridors looking like we were going somewhere. With teachers on the prowl (or, more likely, also on the skive), this became a bit tricky to carry off, especially when you were spotted in the same corridor for the fifth time in half an hour. Being third-formers, we were banned from the school library (only sixth-formers were deemed responsible enough to sit and read), and in that day and age, there was no such thing as a common room – let pupils sit down without working?... God forbid! For a while, we favoured crouching by the brook behind Hut C, until old Plantpot the Geography teacher spotted us and moved us on. If there were no Games on, we could go and hide in the cricket nets, but as the absence of Games usually meant it was raining, this was an uncomfortable option. So for the most part, we just wandered aimlessly around the corridors, two fugitives from the world of science.

Scruff and Fish would have been disconcerted to learn that Snikpoh and I both ended up as engineers (of a kind) in the computer industry, actually producing products people wanted, rather than piffling about with pulleys and pipettes. Neither Scruff nor Fish nor, to be fair, their A-stream charges had any inkling about the technological revolution on the horizon.

LEGS's Art teacher would also find it hard to believe that I subsequently got paid for developing computer illustrations. What a blessing is the computer to the untalented oik! At LEGS I regularly came a distant last in Art exams and for a very particular reason: the Art teacher, who made so little impression on me that I can't even remember her name, but let's call her Farty... Farty had the extraordinary idea that we should be able to make freehand drawings of reality. Knowledge of that handy invention, the camera, had apparently not yet seeped through the granite walls of Long Eaton Grammar School. Though I say so myself, I was in 1963 already a handy wielder of the ubiquitous Brownie, as shown I think in my penetrative study, *Class 4 At Rest* (Figure 7).

Not that my creativity deserted me the moment I picked up a pencil. Snikpoh and I did manage to raise a laugh or two with with our still unpublished series of cartoons entitled *The Thoughts of Arthur Lampkin*, based on the life and times of the scrambling star, and a world exclusive of which appears as Figure 10. Admittedly the only laughs raised were our own, but surely even Gary Larson was the first to laugh at his own creations. *The Thoughts of Arthur Lampkin* were one of the hundred under-the-desk activities that form the main – and possibly only – creative outlet for English schoolboys condemned to sit through six years of mind-numbing offal such as the Julius Caesar and The Corn Laws[18].

To offer a little background, the main sporting interest on Saturday afternoon TV in the 1960s – unless you cared to wait for the ludicrous all-in exploits of Jackie Pallo on ITV at four o'clock – was the scrambling on BBC from 1:35. Before it turned into some Japanese emperor called Maximoto Cross, scrambling was a form of outdoor motor-cycle racing around mud-spattered courses with improbable slopes. The muddiest and best rider was one Arthur Lampkin, and the excitable commentator one Murray Walker, before he took his extraordinary sentence construction to Formula One. The under-the-desk idea was that Snikpoh or I would draw a cross-section of a scrambling course and then pass it to the other, who would draw little motor bikes in perverse positions on this course, with bubbles of frantic speech coming out of the riders' mouths. I remember in one French lesson, where the formation of the pluperfect for some reason failed to hold our attention, one of Snikpoh's captions starting me on

---

[18] Great name for a band.

44

a giggle that wouldn't stop. It showed two riders, one with an absurdly large, semi-circular head. The other rider was saying: "Oy, big 'ead – are you Arfur Lampkin or 'alf a pumpkin?" Interrupted in his rendition of "J'avais fait, tu avais fait, il av .... Guise, what do you think is so funny about the pluperfect, boy?!", Monsieur 'Orobin wrested the offending cartoon from my lap, glanced at it, shook his head and threw it in the bin (the cartoon, not his head). Thus was art treated in LEGS.

In Farty's classes, all my drawings of people were misshapen little stick men and I came bottom. In 'Neddy' Secombe's Woodwork classes, all my bookshelves were misshapen little sticks and I came bottom again. I did actually *try* in Neddy's Woodwork and Metalwork classes though, because I could see some point in being able to make things: saving money, for example. Unfortunately, I had – and still do have – two left hands, ten thumbs and no co-ordination. All I was able to make was Neddy mad. But I maintain to this day that the maddest occasion was his own fault. It was the only time a LEGS teacher actually hit me.

We were learning how metal is pliable when you heat it up. Our little task to prove this was to make a metal milk-bottle top: a handy little gadget for when you lose the original top and don't want some creepy-crawly to worm its way into your pinta. I'll spare you the complex high-tech details that we technological wizards had to incorporate in its design, but in very simple terms this gadget was a round disc with a hollow pushed in the middle. In fact, that's all it was really. You'll have noticed the key words in the design specification: round, hollow, and middle. Now, 3A boys were not exactly God's gift to British industry. The long-suffering Neddy saw plenty of oblong discs emerging from the furnaces, and one triangular one ("Simpkins, you buffoon!"). Mills complained that his finished article had come out upside down ("Turn it round, Mills, you oik!") My particular problem was the "in the middle" bit. While I was punching the hollow into my hot metal disc, my hand slipped and the hollow ended up on the edge of the disc and so I lifted it up on the end of the tongs to show Neddy.

"Look, sir, it's come out lop-sided."

Now I don't know which planet Neddy had just landed from, but it was evidently somewhere with no variation in temperature, for he lifted the white-hot disc off the tongs with his bare fingers. I held my breath. After what seemed like half-an-hour, but must have been a fraction of a second, Neddy let out a baleful moan, threw the disc to the ground, clapped me round the ear, let out another moan and stormed out of the room in the direction of the nurse's office.

During the uncomfortable ten minutes he was gone, we all gathered around the offending object, which was now beginning to cool down, and wondered out loud what could have persuaded Neddy to be so foolish. None could think of any reason why I might be to blame. Eventually, with a violent crash, Mr Secombe burst through the door. We all shrank back behind a bench. He advanced on us, his bandaged hand limp by his side and his eyes fixed on me. With his unbandaged hand, he extracted me from the melée, placed me square in front of him and belted me round the head again, this time with such force that my ears were ringing for the rest of the day. Thus was justice treated in LEGS.

Only boys were allowed to do Woodwork and Metalwork in the politically incorrect 1960s, and only girls to do Cookery. I recently wandered around the battered buildings that once were LEGS and that now are simply Long Eaton School. Peeking through one window, I saw a room full of cookers and fridges, but the sign outside didn't say Cookery – it said "Food Technology Department". They may have gone ape on their language nowadays, but at least I believe the lads now learn how to cook for themselves too. I certainly wish I had, as after 30 years, I'm getting a bit sick of burnt sausage and beans. Among the hundred other basic skills with which the English Grammar School system failed to equip me were how to drive a car, how to write a CV, how to fill in a tax form, how to buy a season ticket at Nottingham Forest, etc. etc. etc. I don't know whether these flaws have been fixed yet. As today's school-leavers can apparently neither write nor spell nor add up, they must be learning *something* else. Perhaps they're learning how not to drown.

The Grange Park Tortures

The LEGS attitude to sport was a strange one.

Children of school age have a natural tendency to run around – hence the constant reminders that we should not run along the corridors. In fact, until an embarrassingly advanced age, I tended to break into a run anywhere – on the way to school, along the High Street, up the street to the chip shop. In the eyes of Mad Ron Barnett, our purpletracksuited sportsmaster, however, we needed to be *taught* how to run, and so winter Wednesday afternoons would often see hundreds of us tearing out of the school gates in our white vests and blue pants, scattering pensioners in our wake as we hurtled along Tamworth Road. But, we'll see later, that was where the hurtling stopped.

Children of school age also have, I have found from experience, a natural tendency to sink when dropped in water. Some basic lessons in how not to drown, therefore, would seem a vital requirement of the education system, but, true to the LEGS teaching ethos, Mad Ron managed to put me off swimming for life. I suspect that, even forty-odd years after the Grange Park Tortures, many other former LEGS inmates are, like me, still non-swimmers.

Every one of the thousands of Long Eatonians to have waded into the sea at Skegness will appreciate that the Arctic Ocean is much nearer to us than the Mediterranean. Now, the combination of Long Eaton's latitude (more or less the same as as Skegness's) and the absence over the first thirty post-war years of heated pools in these parts, combined to create the town's own willy-refrigeration centre. It was located near the present Long Eaton United ground and called Grange Park Baths. During the season laughably referred to as summer, Mad Ron and Even Madder Ronette, would drive whole classloads of victims across town in sealed trucks to Grange Park, there to be herded into grey, concrete changing rooms, prodded like reluctant cattle through ice-cold showers, issued with blow-up water wings to avoid any actual fatalities during school time and forced, shivering with fear, to jump through the pack ice into the torture pool itself.

Personally, I found that clinging onto the side of the pool could keep approximately 25% of my surface area out of the ice floes, so that, when I was finally allowed out after my thirty minutes of hell, part of me was still more or less flesh-coloured. The rest was the colour of those prehistoric remains found in Alpine glaciers: a deathly shade of blue. All our willies had virtually disappeared, and whatever the girls had down there had surely gone the same way.

A later sufferer from the 1970s told me that, on one unusually scorching day during the unusually long, hot summer of 1976, he found the water of the Grange Park Baths to be just on the acceptable side of cool and was foolhardy enough to buy a season ticket. He never used it again.

It was to be over a decade before I discovered that some stretches of the water that covers the Earth's surface maintain a temperature some way above freezing point and that, when male humans enter it in swimming garb, it does not actually freeze their bollocks off. By then, however, it was too late[19]. I never recovered from the Grange Park Tortures and still can't swim, even after several years of living by the very edge of the Mediterranean.

One activity I was actually quite good at was tennis, and so naturally, I wasn't allowed to play it at school – because, apparently, all the tennis places had already been taken. (Was I absent for the auditions?) Another was the one which, as far as we boys were concerned, was the only sport worth devoting any sweat to and that was, of course, Association Football. 90% of us were Nottingham Forest supporters, since our local heroes had recently won the FA Cup[20] and so we all wanted to be another Jack Burkitt or maybe another Roy Dwight with his broken leg. (None of us wanted to be Roy's cousin Reg, since he, like us, was still in short trousers and hadn't yet become Elton John.) The other 10% were Derby County supporters, God help them, but even they knew what our national sport was. Everyone in England knew. Everyone that is except Ron Barnett.

LEGS 3, Nottingham High School 94

Mad Ron was interested only in sports that involved one or more of The Three Ms:

- Mud

- Mayhem

- and Murder

Consequently, when it came to ball games, he had eyes only for that ludicrous Midlands invention with the misshapen ball and the impenetrable rules: rugby union. Ron loved it; we hated it. Ron thought that moving a freezing ball around a frozen pitch was best done with your bare hands; we preferred kicking it. Ron thought that sticking your head between steaming third-form buttocks was fun; we

---

[19] I mean for my swimming, not for my bollocks. Not quite.

[20] A feat they have mysteriously failed to repeat ever since.

thought any physical-contact sport was a bit dodgy. Ron thought he was in Eton; we knew we were in *Long* Eaton.

None of us had the slightest interest in rugby, none had ever visited nor had any intention of visiting a rugby match, and none of us paid any attention whatsoever to Ron's weekly lectures on the Rules of the Game. To this day, when I accidentally see a game on TV, their explanation of any infringement has that 'Chemistry' effect on me: glazed eyes and a lurch for the door. No such luxury was available in LEGS. We were trapped in the changing rooms as Mad Ron droned on and on and on and on about the offside rule, but none of us had a clue what it was. As far as we were concerned the Rules of Rugby Football were very brief:

• Rule 1: Keep as far as possible from that dirty ball.

• Rule 2: Ignore any other rules.

Consequently our Games periods consisted of 30 boys disseminating in a roughly centrifugal manner away from the centre of the rugby field and Ron bawling at us to come back. This happened every Wednesday afternoon for four years. To give you an idea of the abyss within which our rugby playing standard was immutably fixed, even *I* was actually picked for the school team.

My mistake had been to spot the one position on a rugby field where you never have to get involved in those nasty-looking scrummages and from where, if you squinted your eyes a bit, you could almost imagine you were playing *real* football. That position is Full Back, and my preference for it had unfortunately given Ron the impression that I was developing it into something of a speciality. So one day I was picked to play against Friesland School on a Saturday morning. I refused. I was dragged in front of Old Man Grimes, the headmaster, who was forced to acknowledge that the only obligation to attend school on Saturdays was for detention. My card, however, was duly marked.

Despite my escape, Mad Ron didn't give up. He really must have been either crashingly stupid or desperate or both, but he nailed me for an evening fixture against Nottingham High School, who – rumour had it – actually knew how to play the game. Rumour was right. Playing at home, we lost 3 - 94.

This is the absolute truth. The three points came when the ball accidentally struck Michael Simpkins in the stomach. He'd been loitering about near the opposition's line and, under the impact, fell over and trapped the ball under his body. He was still winded when mobbed by the rest of us: even if you hate the game, scoring is still a bit special. For the LEGS XV it was also unique.

LEGS's rugby field was across the Erewash Canal from the school, on West Park, which also functioned as Long Eaton's flood overflow area. Consequently, rugby was impossible for several weeks each winter – even Mad Ron wasn't mad enough to consign us to a watery grave: he had much more punishment up his sleeve before he would actually let his captives escape through death. One of these alternative punishments conveniently incorporated two of The Three Ms without resort to any school facilities, underwater or otherwise. So, in bleakest midwinter, we would spend Wednesday afternoons on Ron's Runs.

The technical name for this 'sport' is cross-country running, but, countryside being in short supply around Long Eaton, we did cross-*town* running. Ron would sketch out the route on a blackboard in the hall. I think he must have learnt his map-chalking skill from old Plantpot[21], and it was his only worthwhile one. After a lot of stick-beating around the ominous red line that ran through vast tracts of industrial England, Ron asked for questions.

Simpkins: "Sir, what's the scale of the map, sir?"

Ron: "If you ever make it back, Simpkins, you'll know. Next question."

Me: "Sir, where the red line crosses the blue brook, I don't think there's a bridge, sir."

Ron: "That's right, Guise. Next question."

Me again, not knowing when to shut up: "But, sir, 'ow wigunna gerracrossi' then?"

Ron, fists clenched: "How tall are you, Guise?"

Me: "Four foot seven, sir." Giggles break out around me. "But I'm not the shortest – Mills is even smaller than me, sir."

Ron: "You'll get through all right, Guise. Keep your nose up. Mills, see me afterwards. Any more questions? No? Right, off you go, lads – and remember: *no* walking and *no* stopping at tuck shops. I've got spies in the streets!"

---

[21] Ken Plampin, the Geography teacher, benefitted from the most harmless nickname in the school.

I never spotted any of Ron's infamous Spy Squad, so most of us trotted along at a brisk pace until, rounding the corner into Broad Street, we'd adopt a languorous saunter for the rest of the 'run', chatting and taking short cuts where we could. After all, Ron really was a bit naïve if he thought he knew the town's back twitchells better than a pack of 13-year olds. Just before the school buildings swung into sight again, we'd muddy our knees and shirts a bit and then stagger along with theatrical panting across the school yard and into the steaming showers.

Any road up, despite Mad Ron's earnest endeavours, he didn't quite put me off running for life. At the ripe old age of 35 I finally overcame the Barnetian traumas and once again put trainer to pavement. Or rather, put trainer where rubber plimsoll had once trodden. Thus duly kitted out, I joined a running club that every Thursday night slogged around the lanes of a village not a million miles from Long Eaton, on real cross-country runs. Mad Ron would be shocked to learn that I actually entered a race and ran five miles around Donington Park motor-racing circuit. Without stopping – at a tuck shop or anywhere else.

The Alternative Sports Day

The highlight of the Barnetian year was Sports Day. This was an opportunity for Mad Ron and Even Madder Ronnette to inveigle the rest of the staff into their imperial adventures. The purple pair would march about for the entire afternoon, clipboards in hand, dishing out stopwatches by the dozen to their battalion of colleagues, barking out orders by the hundred to an army of prefects, always gleaming that manic sports-teacher gleam that many an unathletic urchin such as myself learned quickly to be wary of.

The key to the proceedings on Sports Day was your house: not as in bricks and mortar, but as in the English tradition of assigning inmates of educational establishments to mythical 'houses'. This is supposed to foster a sense of belonging and encourage a spirit of healthy competition. LEGS's three houses were Trent, Derwent and Soar. I assume that Long Eaton's own river, the Erewash, in whose valley it sits and whose name is given to the local dialect shared with the old mining towns to the north, was excluded on grounds of southern snobbery. Or because the headmaster thought that no-one may feel inclined to be part of something that the BBC regularly pronounced as 'ear wash'[22]. I was in Trent house and you won't be surprised to learn that I had no intention of feeling part of it. Like many other inmates, the only emotion I could summon up about LEGS was the anticipated joy of leaving it – and dividing LEGS into three didn't make any difference. I'm pleased to relate that, throughout my six-year sentence I didn't contribute a single sporting point to Trent House. I didn't even compete in a single event on any Sports Day. Except the Alternative Sports, that is...

LEGS's Alternative Sports Day in June 1968 was not my idea, though I wish it had been. In the year of *Jumpin' Jack Flash*, I was in the Lower Sixth and it was a group of brave *Upper* Sixth-Formers who started the underground proposal that those of us underwhelmed by the whole idea of school sports should, the day before Sports Day, decamp at lunchtime to the sports field and enjoy ourselves. (Mad Ron wouldn't have understood this concept.) Amongst the events were:

• Freestyle Pillow Fighting
• The Blindfold Hundred Yards
• The Short Jump
• and The Four-Legged Race

No points were to be awarded to anyone for anything and winners were to be decided by a show of hands. The Blindfold Hundred Yards, for example, went not to the first across the line, but to Michael Simpkins, who had to be rescued just before he ran headlong into the canal. I can't stop myself telling you that I was in the winning team of the Four-Legged Race. My two partners in ropes were Bill Bass and Kevin Trapp, both six-footers. Being in the middle, I had no control over either leg and understand that we were awarded victory on the grounds that, against all odds, I had incurred no permanent injury.

After a lot of fun, word eventually reached the Head's ears, as it were, and we were unceremoniously ushered off the field and back to school. Scandalously, our brave ringleaders got detentions for misuse of school property and we mere supporters were let off, although I notice that, given also my lack of devotion to the fortunes

---

[22] The correct pronunciation is Errywash, as in Errywash the Wake.

of the LEGS rugby team, I was never made even a sub-prefect. Your loss, Grimesy me old mate!

A Spring Too Far

Before we leave the sad, sad world of school sports, I must justify my claim that the female half of the Purple Pairing from Pinxton was even madder than the male. For one gym period, Mad Ronnette was entrusted with both halves of 3A and had boys and girls running, jumping, diving and bouncing around the gym like there was no tomorrow. One little stunt into which we were coerced was to run at full pelt towards a horizontal bar placed high off the ground and then, just before arrival, to jump two-footed onto a kind of springboard. The speed of our moving bodies was supposed to see us soaring upward and onward until, *en passant*, we would grab hold of said bar, hang there like a side of beef for a few seconds and then, when Mad Ronnette finally gave us the OK, fall to earth.

She asked a couple of us to make some trial runs while she adjusted the position of the springboard. On my first pass, I ran, bounced, soared, missed the bar completely and landed several yards ahead of the drop zone with a resounding thud that broke my arm. I knew I'd broken it, having managed to do so twice before – same arm, same place. Pain was somehow subsumed under the urgent need to draw Mad Ronette's attention to what had happened, as she was busy driving the rest of the lemmings to their violent fate. I bustled over to her and raised my good arm.

"Er, Miss Barnett – I mean Mrs Barnett – I've broken my arm."

"What's that, Guise?"

"I've broken my arm, Miss. I've done it before and so I ..."

"Oh, stop moaning, boy, and get in line."

So I trudged over to the line, where I vouchsafed to Hopkins, who was ahead of me: "I've broken my arm, Snikpoh. Honest." Snikpoh thought this was a pretty good joke and ran off to do his bit. Mad Ronnette adjusted the board and beckoned for me to go next.

"I've ...", I started, but saw the futility of it.

So, beginning to cry now, in frustration as well as pain, I ran off, bounced half-heartedly on the board, soared on a very low trajectory beneath the bar, my good arm pathetically outstretched above my head, until I used it to break my fall. My wince on landing and

53

failure to get up finally drew The Mad One over. Seeing my now-swelling left elbow, she got the message.

"All right, Guiso, you'd better go home and get it sorted out."

So much for the caring teacher. The female of the species is, I maintain, madder than the male.

A Memory Like a Sieve With No Holes

Now, those of you paying any attention at all to this rather biased overview of life at LEGS may have noticed a disparity between my claim to have subsequently sailed through university and the hard fact that I came bottom, or very nearly so, in all the practical subjects so far covered. This mismatch is explained by my position at or near the top in all the *im*practical subjects. The middle ground is territory I never saw.

Not that I actually *understood* anything in these subjects – Geography, History, German, French[23] etc. – no, no, that would have been most pretentious and would probably have resulted in my immediate expulsion. After all, the last thing that any LEGS teacher wanted was for their pupils to understand what they were talking about – good grief, there'd be nothing left to distinguish the teachers from the pupils! No, all they asked was that we pupils *memorized* what they said and more especially memorized what they wrote on the blackboard. With a head as empty as mine, this was a piece of cake.

Even now, I can see Plantpot's beautifully chalked cross-section of the Atacama Desert. (I still intend to go there to see if the Pacific is really as blue as it was on Hut C's blackboard.) I can still see Miss Cantor's finely scrawled list of The Causes of The First World War in Room 4. (I mean the list was in Room 4 – I think the war itself took place somewhere else, but we never got that far).

Miss Cantor also taught Divinity – an interesting idea, being taught how to assume the mantle of divineness. I wish we'd also been taught some of God's other tricks: invisibility and omnipresence, for example. Of course, given the C of E's own omnipresence in 1960s

---

[23] Although the ability to speak another language is a very practical asset, such a skill was not actually one of the rewards from a language course at LEGS – see later.

Long Eaton (see later), no other contenders for divinity were ever going to get a look-in except The Big J, whose life was full of dates and places for us to memorise:

0 AD.[24]	Born, haystack, Bethlehem.
14 - 30 AD.	Educated, assorted deserts. (No qualifications)
31 - 33 AD.	Persecuted, assorted market places. (I always wondered what 'persecuted' meant, but never had the courage to ask.)
34 AD.	Died... or did he? (Discuss)

A Successful Cheater's Guide to Cheating

Give me a list of dates and a few chalky old maps and you'll have me sailing through the exams in no time – divine or not. It was even a doddle to cheat. For any students with exam nerves, I recommend the following simple yet effective devices:

- For those tricky little data that just won't lodge in the old grey matter (e.g. the annual rainfall figure at Cherrapunji), try writing them in red biro on your wooden ruler, next to the names of your favourite pop groups. Since the latter include the likes of 'Unit 4 Plus 2' and 'The DC 5', any nosy adjudicator will naturally assume that '154 inches' were just another one-hit wonder.

- For really complicated stuff (e.g. the formula for a standard deviation), write it at the top of pages 12 and 13 of your log tables – you'll never have them open by accident.

- For bigger lumps of cheating (e.g. the 14 Consequences of the Civil War), just write them in blue biro on your blotter and then, if the adjudicator gets suspicious, stick your fountain pen in the middle of the blotter and, lo and behold, the Consequences of the Civil War will have disappeared.

What do you mean, you've never seen a wooden ruler? You don't know what log tables are?! You've never used a fountain pen?!! God, no wonder half the kids today leave school without any qualifications. If you can't even cheat at school, what chance have you got in the real world?

---

[24] Remarkable coincidence that.

6. Christmas at Brooklands School, probably 1958. I appear to be the only boy in the class, but it's just a trick of the light. Is that our headmaster, with the suspiciously red nose?
   Photo: Horace Holme

7. Class 4 At Rest. Brooklands' senior class visits Regent's Park Zoo, London, 1962/3. What teacher was brave enough to take this lot out for the day?! *Photo: author*

8. The eastern entrance to Long Eaton Grammar School, one sunny day in the 1960s. Surprisingly little has changed in the subsequent 30+ years: the gates are still there, though the curved walls, their sawn-off iron railings already long gone for wartime use at the time of this photograph, have since been straightened. Miss Bottom's form-room (for 1A and 2A) was Room 4 on the ground floor, partially hidden here behind the central tree trunk.

Photo: John Sumpter, reproduced by kind permission of Sumpter's, the Image Makers

9. Grange Park Baths, scene of The Grange Park Tortures. This 1960s shot shows suspiciously more people outside the water than in it. It's now an indoor bowling centre and no doubt has some form of heating. *Photo: Albert Towlson*

10. World-exclusive extraxt from *The Thoughts of Arthur Lampkin*, a series of under-the-desk cartoons drawn during the more boring lessons at Long Eaton Grammar School (viz. any of them) by Ian Hopkins and the author. © *I. Hopkins and R. Guise, 1964 (probably)*

61

3

Ah Yes, the Irksome Four

Sorry, I've been rambling. So far I've mentioned only the Irksome One: school.

I distinctly remember making a mental list of the activities I wanted – and intended – to get out of my life. The list occurred to me while trudging through a windswept and deserted Long Eaton Market Place one Wednesday morning in 1964, at around 8:35 a.m.. The reason I can pinpoint it is that this trudge was from one of the ghastly activities into which I'd been press-ganged, to another. I remember the leaves and the puddles, and Therm House drifting past on my left, as it occurred to me that I might just possibly have some modicum of control over my life. You get these moments from time to time in your life, don't you? When you're suddenly elevated above the daily grind and see yourself in a broader context where different routes suddenly become discernible. In this 1964 instance, I decided that my control would henceforth be focussed on ridding myself of The Irksome Four. I didn't call them that at the time, but have since discovered that objectives with labels are much more likely to be achieved than those without, and since I did, ultimately, nine years later on a glorious day in the Summer of '75, near a southern Cotswold escarpment, achieve the goal of final disengagement from the last of the list... I hereby retrospectively name these indignities 'The Irksome Four'.

But what were they? Apart from another jolly good name for a band, they were: School, Church, Piano Lessons, and Cubs. The first to go was Cubs.

Arkaila and the Woggle Boys

At some stage, for some reason and most probably at some expense, it was announced that I was going to join the Cubs. To be precise, I was going to join the 10th Long Eaton Cub Scouts.

Now, I was not what anyone would have described as a robust child, and no doubt the Cubs were supposed to toughen me up – a laudable aim, but one which I instinctively resisted. With the Cubs, there lay before me the ghastly prospect of camps and tents and fires and singing... and goodness knows what other grimness. However, I'm very pleased to report that I managed to emerge from the Cubs without ever having poked my woggle-clad neck outside the hut on St John's Street; I wonder if there are any other completely camp-free ex-Cubs out there? My entire two-year Cub Scout career passed in a Friday-night blur of indoor running, indoor knot-tying, indoor allegiances to God, Queen and Country, and general indoor dib-dib-dibbing. Resisting the ethos at almost very turn, I successfully avoided not only every camp but also the award of a single badge; are there any other completely *badge*-free ex-Cubs out there? Yes, even my reef-knots were so inept that the right sleeve of my green woolly jumper remained a virginal badge-free zone.

The left sleeve, though, did not remain a *stripe*-free zone, for the Cubs, like life in general, were organized as a hierarchy. At the top was God, just below whom – or maybe even at the right-hand side of whom – was Queen Elizabeth II, below whom was Arkaila, a roly-poly woman who held sway over the troop, and below or at the side of or even tucked in behind whom was an enigmatic red-faced figure called Bruce. At the top of the pile of Cubs that milled around below these pillars of society were the Sixers, each of whom was in charge of a six-pack of other Cubs. Should a Sixer be absent, his deputy, the Seconder, smartly took the reins. Below the Seconders was a mass of standard-issue snotty little Cubs.

Now, earning a little badge by demonstrating that I could rub two sticks together on some damp Derbyshire moor to which I hadn't the slightest intention of letting myself be consigned, represented for me little incentive compared with the prospect of lording it over my fellow urchins with the aid of the two magical yellow stripes that denoted a Sixer. So, while successfully avoiding any rough stuff, I did assiduously follow every indoor, Friday-night command issued by Bruce or Arkaila or the Queen or God, and thus rapidly gained promotion to the rank of Sixer. I was thus put in charge of as disorderly a rabble of gits as you might ever find. The only pleasure I recall during my short – and only – stint of service to the Queen was to harry and prod my sloppy and unco-ordinated Six into something akin to a straight line; and then to stand ramrod-rigid at the head of this line, the two yellow stripes quivering on my left arm, and the strains of *Rule Britannia* humming emotionally through my inflated head. (I'm pretty sure my republicanism started the next day… if only I'd have known what that anti-Queen feeling was called, which I didn't.)

Cub Scouts were one thing, but your actual Boy Scouts would have been quite another. Somehow I managed to get midad to grant me an honourable discharge before I was fired. As I returned to civvies, The Irksome Four became The Irksome Three.

John, Paul, George and the Multi-Tailed Tadpoles

In our front room we had a piano, with a revolving piano stool in front and photographs of my four grandparents on top. It was the only musical instrument in the house and, since everyone could play it, it came as no surprise that I was going to be despatched every Monday evening at half past six to Mrs Paling's house on Charlton Avenue, with my leather music case, half a crown and ten uncontrollable fingers.

Now, my three years of learning music coincided with the decline of The Big O and the rise of The Fab Four, both in my record-buying and in my soul, where they still reside. Although the English musical renaissance of the 1960s was more than 'just' The Beatles – honourable mentions must go to The Kinks, The Hollies, Manfred Mann and a few more – those four blokes from Liverpool were just, well, to use a phrase popular at the time, 'something else'. From the confident "da-da-da-deeeedideedi" of *Please Please Me* to the self-mocking "And I hope we pass the audition" of *Get Back*, I was well and truly, hero-worshippingly, record-collectingly, lyric-memorizingly, every-move-observingly hooked. Those short periods when I knew there was a new Beatles single due, but hadn't yet heard it, were so unspeakably tantalizing that I would pass them in some kind of trance. Every new track was, just, well, fantastic[25]! Even 35

---

[25] C'von, ovontually, *Revolution No. 9,*

years on, it looks like my vocabulary just hasn't got the words to convey how good, how original, how overwhelming their music was. The measure is that, after listening to any Beatles CD now, I still wonder why I ever bothered listening to anyone else. It's all there.

The front room at 10 Charlton Avenue, Long Eaton, however, was strangely immune to these developments. Mrs Paling's choice of composers to bring out my latent musical talent consisted solely of dead Germans. While, just down the M1 at Watford, an equally short, shy youth, with similar stubby little fingers, was hammering out the blues for Bluesology, I was stumbling through a Fugue in F for Mrs P. I'm not saying I could have rivalled Elton John – to start with, I had no actual talent – just that some incentive might have urged me to practise a little more. Incentive like music with a bit of rhythm, for example. Or even a tune. As it was, my practices became fewer and farther between as the lessons dragged on, until it was painfully obvious to Mrs P that I hadn't even looked at the piece she'd given me to learn seven days before. It was obvious because I never got the hang of that so-called sight-reading (as though a braille-reading pianist was a practical alternative).

You don't have to be a budding Beethoven to spot that the music on a piano keyboard comes from a series of black and white oblongs, with the scale arranged horizontally; whereas the music on a sheet of paper comprises a series of black and white tadpoles, with the scale arranged vertically. A black tadpole on the paper does not necessarily represent a black oblong on the piano; nor a white tadpole a white oblong. Why this weird design for written music was even invented, let alone accepted, is a mystery. I, for one, found it hard enough to get my fingers to hit the right oblongs, without having to do a simultaneous mental translation from symbolic multi-tailed tadpoles.

However, I do thank Mrs P for trying her hardest with the rawest of raw material, and midad for forking out yet more dosh on my cultural development. Once or twice, instead of 6/8 on a record, I invested two bob of my 10/- pocket money on sheet music; fifteen years later I bought my own piano; and even now I can still, after a couple of beers, belt out a fault-strewn but atmospheric version of The Moody Blues' *Go Now*. Otherwise, the piano is just a tall, shiny table in the corner.

Nevertheless, having passed a couple of piano exams, I'd knocked one more off and by, the age of fifteen, it was down to The Irksome Two.

Almighty and the Plateman

In Long Eaton in the 1950s, God was alive and well and hovering just above the clouds without any obvious means of support. He was clearly a close relation of Father Christmas: both of them being fat old men with a tendency to lurk around in the sky. While Father Christmas had reindeer, God had angels – which always seemed a rough deal for him[26], since these angels looked like a right bunch of pansies who could barely lift their own harps, let alone do any real work. Maybe it was just as well that God didn't get the gift-distribution franchise, since I couldn't see those cherubic angels pulling a sledge laden with ten tons of presents from Lapland to Long Eaton. God also had a right-hand man called Jesus, who seemed to spend most of his time walking around with a plate behind his head, waving at people. This Jesus, we were often told, "suffocated little children", which didn't seem to me a very nice thing to do, especially if you were supposed to be Saviour of Mankind.

You will have gathered that, as a seven-year-old Sunday School pupil at Top Wesleyan Methodist Church[27], I wasn't too impressed with this God team. My favourite team at the time, you may recall, was The Lone Ranger and Tonto, whose daring deeds I saw in glorious black and white at the Palace cinema every Saturday morning, with another rip-roaring episode on telly at teatime. When Sunday morning came round, and I was still in Hi-Ho-Silver-galloping-down-the-entry mood, you can imagine that, compared to the masked man and his surly sidekick, God and Jesus didn't seem much cop. In fact, if you'd have asked me – which nobody did – they needed a facelift.

For a start, Jesus had to get rid of that plate – I mean, nobody's going to believe you'll save the world with a piece of Spode behind your ears. And, well, I know he made a lot of rousing speeches, but there wasn't exactly much *action*. What Jesus needed was a *weapon*: a sword maybe, like Zorro – yes, the White Avenger with his handy rapier. Now we were getting somewhere. But what about the God

---

[26] We'll skip the He and Him business, shall we?

[27] I never did discover what it was on top of.

character? Well, I liked the name, it sounded impressive and I liked the way that it was Dog spelt backwards. Maybe his sidekick should be another pet spelt backwards. Tac? No, that sounded stupid. Eigdub? No. Ragiregdub? Yes, that's it: God and Ragiregdub, the White Avenger. And what about that Holy Ghost? He was always getting a mention but he never actually *did* anything. Now I come to think of it, you never actually *saw* him in any pictures either. Well, he was a ghost after all... yes, we could work on that. If he was invisible, the Holy Ghost could get God and Raggy out of some pretty tricky situations. What about that bit when the Romans nailed Jes .. I mean, nailed Raggy to that cross? Just as he's fading away, the camera could zoom in to the nails and see them being mysteriously pulled out by some ghostly pliers wielded by the Holy Ghost. Raggy jumps to the ground, the Invisible One throws him his sword, and he sets about the villainous Romans, just holding out till God charges up on his stallion with his merry band of angels .,, no, those cissy angels would have to go they could be a band of dwarves instead God charges up with his merry band of dwarves with their merry catapults, and they pelt the Romans with thousands of merry stones until they're all dead or running away, and then the dwarves carry Raggy off on their shoulders ... into the sunset. Dangdadalang… dadalangdadalang… dadaDADA!

These Sunday School teachers had no idea. All Mrs MacDougal told us was something about Pascal the Lamb, and not even any sign of his mate Larry. I remember one lesson where we were all supposed to be praying, hands clasped together and heads bowed low, and Mrs Mac caught me staring up at the ceiling.

"What are you thinking about, Richard?," she asked in that sickeningly tender voice that mothers use to other people's children, perhaps supposing I was in mid-appeal to God for some particularly important help.

"I wuz jus' thinkin' it's a long time since The Bumblies 've bin on, Miss."

"The what? On what?"

God, didn't she know *anything?* "The Bumblies on the telly, Miss. You know, on *It's a Square World* wiv Michael Bentine, when them little Bumblies come on that lives on the ceilin'."

I don't think Mrs MacDougal rated my chances in Heaven, even then. She'd have been surprised to see me ten years later floating around in cassock and surplice, swinging the old incense for all I was worth. But that's what I somehow got into. Not 'got into' in the hippy all-consuming-hobby sense, but 'got into' in the accidental how-can-I-get-out-of-this? sense.

This transformation was down to the family's allegiance being transferred, for what reason I don't recall, from Top Wesleyan to Long Eaton's parish church, St Laurence's. Here the services were what I subsequently discovered is called High Church and were as near to Catholic as dammit is to swearing, that is to say, even more ridiculous than in other churches. Not that I was allowed to give voice to such blasphemous views at the time of course. From my initial tie-clad, waist-high position next to whichever family member went to St Laurence's on a Sunday morning, it just looked like the same boring old drill as at Top Wesleyan: lines of grown-ups bouncing up and down between feet, bum and knees, while droning some God-awful dirges about "Thou art" this and "Lord help us with" the other. Lord help us indeed. With *The Navy Lark* on the Home Service at two, the sooner it was all over the better.

Gurgle Gurgle Waaah

For those not up on these things, I should explain what the C of E is. Or rather was. The Church of England was a religious cult that was rife on a north European island, from the 16th century to the start of the 21st. The C of E theoretically worshipped a first-century Jewish prophet, but overtly ignored all his teaching, even as it was reported in their sacred book, *The Minutes of the Parochial Church Council Meetings, 1544 to 2003*. The C of E's real agenda was to control the hearts and minds of the English people, thereby keeping them quiescent and governable for their cohorts: the English Kings, Queens and, later, Conservative Party Central Office. This they achieved in spectacular fashion, by the following means:

- They caught their prey young, usually around the age of three months, by initiating the precocious youngsters in a 'baptism' ceremony. Here the babe would affirm he had reflected seriously on the meaning of life, had investigated the claims and counter-claims of the major world religions of the day, and had come to the inevitable conclusion that a first-century Jewish hippy (Christ, J) was the son of an overweight but otherwise supernatural cloud-hovering guru, who would watch over him (the reflective infant) for the rest of his life. Or, as it usually came out: "Gurgle gurgle waaaah dribble". In 1952, I personally pronounced this solemn oath: "Gagagaga thpthpthpfaaaart".

- Understanding the power of statistics, the C of E kept a record of the number of baptisms all across England. Unfortunately, no equivalent ceremony was[28] available for any subsequent denial of faith: an anti-baptism as it were – "When I said 'Gurgle gurgle waaaah dribble', I'm afraid that's exactly what I meant, and hereby apologise for any misunderstanding and statistical error that I may have caused, so help me God" – and so the figures for believers just grew and grew. Eventually people referred to England as a Christian *country*, as though not only the dribbling babes but also the very soil professed religious belief: "St Botolph's was quite full that Easter, with all the local hyacinths turning out in their Sunday best, the newly cropped privet hedges filling two whole rows at the front, and a visiting mountain ash (who was spending the weekend with the Deacon Hills) booming a tuneful baritone to *And Did Those Feet ...*"

- The C of E also managed to inveigle itself into the English constitution – or rather into the ragbag of laws that passed as a constitution in this backward land. The reigning monarch had to be C of E – nowadays a detail of little significance outside the gossip columns, but 400 years ago, when monarchs actually did things (cut off citizens' heads, for example), being the loyal subject of some lunatic who might at any moment appoint a hyacinth as Bishop of Gloucester was at best a vulnerable position. Even in the early 21st century, laws had to be given the OK by a second house infested by bishops, ex-bishops, ex-choristers, ex-Conservative-party-chairmen and other half-wits.

The net effect of this insidious campaign was that the simple citizen – including a Long Eaton teenager before he saw the light – subconsciously held God, the Queen and England to be more or less the same thing, viz. that thing represented by the Union Jack, the thing that two world wars were fought for, the thing that the Last Night of the Proms evoked, and the thing that overcame West

---

[28] Until recently. You can now complete a 'Declaration of De-Baptism' form, available from the National Secular Society at www.secularism.org.uk.

Germany in extra time at Wembley. The fact that I now know God to be a lie, the Queen to be a rock group and only England to be real, does not detract from the years of imposed deception at the hands of the C of E. Such tricks are beneath contempt ... but perhaps not beneath the law? I wonder if I could sue the Church of England for "wilfully filling the head of a susceptible minor with blatant untruths, unnecessary guilt and other fabrications, with the express intent of confining him within a cold and unhealthy environment for up to five hours per week, and there extracting moneys, in the form of cash and unpaid labour, to the total over a five-year period of £432 10s 6d."?

Claude's Army

Back in 1964, however, I just did what I was told. Which was a shame really, because at the age of thirteen the C of E puts you through a 'confirmation' ceremony, where you confirm that "Gurgle gurgle waaaah dribble" really did mean "I believe in one God etc." I just said what they told me to, the Bishop of Derby duly put his hands on my head, and I thereby got permission to kneel in front of some medieval icons and let an old man feed me a little white wafer representing the body of a 2000-year-old Jewish hippy. I am not making this up.

After the ceremony I was recruited into Claude's Army.

St Laurence's had a vicar, a well-educated old buffoon called the Rev. William Henry Cannington-Smythe. From his double-barrelled name and his accent, it was pretty clear that he wasn't from round our way. The Rev was God's local rep and, like me, just turned up when he was told and did what he was told. Our church was actually run by one Claude Daykin and it was Claude who did most of the telling. I assume he was the second Son of God and that his real name was Claude Christ. Certainly he acted like the Messiah, floating around in his long black cassock with no obvious means of support, beaming his beatific smile. And certainly everyone did what Claude told them. I don't actually remember seeing the plate behind his head, nor hearing his name in any of the chants we had to learn ("Holy Mary, mother of Claude ...etc."), but his divinity was there between the lines all right. Officially I think he was called a Churchwarden and Master of Servers.

Claude ran the church services and they ran like clockwork. He had at his disposal a vast army of well-drilled Soldiers of Christ, five of

71

whom were selected each week as the Sunday Morning Battalion to take control of the strategically important 10:45 service. The five were:

- *The Master of Ceremonies* (I swear I am not making this up), who acted as the Commander on the day and who was often General Daykin himself.

- *Two Acolytes*, who moved around in perfect symmetry carrying two candles, but whose real role was to shepherd the Rev into the right position at the right time. (The Rev was not really up to the same drill standard as the rest of us, finding regular excuses to miss Claude's crucial practice sessions). The acolytes had the added responsibility of auxiliary firemen in case the Rev's chasuble caught fire, which, with so many naked flames on and around the altar, it sometimes did. I remember one service after which Claude berated me for having used the Rev's own holy-water-sprinkler to put out just such a potential inferno in the Rev's vestments. Just doing my duty, Your Claudeness.

- *One Thurifer*, who throughout the service held his left hand clasped to his breast and, in his right, a chain, at the end of which swung another constant fire hazard: the thurible. The thurible was stacked full of foul-smelling incense which had to be set alight in the vestry at precisely 10:43, kept topped up for the entire service and, at pre-defined points in the drill, swung with zeal into the faces of the audience – sorry, congregation. A stock of incense followed the thurifer around in a little golden boat, held by a little golden *Boat Boy*, who was the fifth and last member of the Sunday Morning Battalion.

The Boat Boy's role was to follow the Thurifer wherever he went; the Thurifer's role was not to lose the diminutive Boat Boy, who was often Claude's diminutive son, Holy Paul – the Son of the Son of God, as it were. The smell of the incense really was appalling and I've since discovered that I was and am allergic to it, which would explain my constant red eyes and runny nose during virtually my entire five years in Claude's Army.

I remember another service where, as thurifer, I'd lit up on cue at 10:43, just before the army and the choir were due to make their dramatic entrance into the church from the vestry, when we realized that the Rev wasn't there. Claude, who was MC that day, lifted his cassock to his knees and charged across Long Eaton Market Place to the vicarage, there to wrench the Rev out of bed, while back at base, the organist improvised while I tried to douse the thurible with a surplus surplice. A recently ignited pile of incense, however, is a potent enemy and the infernal fumes began to fill the vestry. The choirmen were all coughing, Claude's Army was on its knees, and tears were streaming down my face, when an apologetic Rev was finally bundled in by Claude, whose own fuming seemed to blind him to the state of the vestry. He bounded up the steps that led to the back of the organ, gave the organist the nod, and charged down again to swing open the vestry doors. To the tune of *Oh Lord on High*, we crashed out into the church amid a billowing cloud of incense which quickly engulfed the congregation. Had they been able to see through the fumes, they would have caught a rare glimpse of Claude's Army in complete disarray: the acolytes feeling their way round the pulpit, their candles lurching dangerously and spilling drops of hot wax onto the clasped hands of the front-row faithful; a red-eyed thurifer peering through tears of agony in search of a boat boy crawling on the floor in a bid for freedom; and the master of ceremonies, Claude himself, staring in bewilderment at the battered state of his battalion. As the fumes cleared I saw a congregation, not laughing or even smirking, but rather burying their heads in their hymn books in utter embarrassment. Unlike real Catholics, these pretend Catholics at the C of E had not one iota of humour. They seemed to be obeying an 11th commandment: thou shalt not laugh.

Laughter was also banned at Claude's practice sessions[29]. This was a tough restriction, not only because of their ludicrous content but also because I was not the only one to look askance on Claude's sham shenanigans. A fellow Grammar Grub, Robert Mooney, had also been conscripted into Claude's Army and had become my best friend. Teenage years have their problems and a constant undercurrent of giggles in the company of friends is one of them. Many of Claude's famous practices took place in his suburban Sawley home, and it's a mystery how Mooney and I got through them without being excommunicated for taking the Lord's living room in vain.

---

[29] I still have my own notes from one of these sessions (goodness knows why). They include such dodgy instructions as "Good Friday. Acolyte 2. When choirmen go down for passion, turn towards them and kneel and rise as appropriate." I think I'd better burn them.

Being invited to the Messiah's home should have been quite an occasion and I suppose the disciples should have walked there on the surface of the Erewash Canal, but we usually went on our bikes. On being invited in, Mooney usually went straight on a surreptitious reckie to see if Claude's daughter Hermione was around, in a perennially unsuccessful attempt to chat her up. Trying to get off with a granddaughter of God seemed to me a potentially heavy engagement and so, while waiting for the others, I'd usually just hang around in the living room looking at the family photos. As Claude hadn't yet acquired a plate, he was difficult to pick out amongst the ramblers in the Peak District. One picture, however, depicted a youth standing on a knoll a little above the others, pointing in the general direction of Macclesfield, and I expect later generations may read of this Sermon on the Knoll. Another seemed to show a group around a large table in a Matlock Bath beer garden and was already entitled The Last Pint.

In civilian life this Son of God was not a carpenter, but a University technician, which meant he had access to the latest modern gadgets, which he could borrow and bring home. In the 1960s this meant that sensational product of Mr Wilson's white hot technology, the Overhead Projector, or "Oh, HP" as we learnt to praise it.

When all the troops had assembled, we gathered round the Oh, HP in the Son of God's living room. Claude took down some of the photos to leave an area of white bobbly wallpaper as the screen. The lights were dimmed and the Oh, HP switched on. We saw a pattern of black lines and shading that formed a detailed map of the business end of St Laurence's: the altar, the choir stalls, the pulpit and the little doors to the sacristy and vestry. Claude had two more maps: one of the entire church, for when the army spilled over into the small Lady Chapel (a small chapel called Lady, not a chapel for small ladies) and one showing the church, the Market Place and the surrounding streets – this for Easter Sunday or Remembrance Sunday, when Claude's Army led the entire congregation on a banner-waving street procession, rather like the Trades Unions or the IRA. If, on one of these extraordinary extra-ecclesiastical escapades, a sniper had decided to start shooting at us (a frustrated motorist, for example), we'd only have had ourselves to blame.

Onto one or other of these maps, Claude would carefully place his *pièces de résistance*: a miniature army of tiny little cardboard cut-outs, each representing one of us: a little candle symbol for an

74

acolyte, a little thurible for the thurifer, a tiny little yacht for the tiny little boat boy, and so on. In the intimate atmosphere of the Son of God's living room, we'd wait with bated breath as Claude named each one of us in turn, simultaneously placing our symbolic image in a precise position on the Oh, HP. These tiny little soldiers would appear like magic as crudely shaped black blobs on the wallpaper, until, when all were in place, Claude would place in the corner of the Oh, HP a giant letter A, which would appear elongated on the ceiling above our heads, in order to instill into our poor little mortal brains that this was Position A: The Start of the Service.

By the time the giant A loomed over us, Mooney and I would be in a parlous state of suppressed whimpers. I'd be biting my knuckles, not daring to look at him, because we both knew what was coming next. The essence of a good service was smooth and co-ordinated movement from one position to the next. To represent this movement on the wallpaper, Claude needed a tiny brass dustpan – a dustpan which lived next to the fireplace and which, if he'd forgotten it, was ceremoniously passed forward to Our Lord at the Altar, I mean Our Claude at the Oh, HP. Then, with all the care of a three-year-old playing on the floor, Claude would use this dustpan to push his little soldiers around the map. We'd see this enormous black shape loom up on the wallpaper, move around and then disappear, to reveal that the Rev, say, had been moved into the pulpit, that is, down by the Son of God's light switch.

It was simultaneously magic and manic. Again and again the black dustpan loomed, and again and again a little Servant of Christ had been moved across the wall, until finally a giant B appeared on the ceiling. Sometimes, Mooney or I had to excuse ourselves, and, outside in the hall, you'd hear the banging of teenage head against wall.

Claude himself seemed oblivious to any of these distractions, conducting these practice sessions in a mood of intense concentration, as the large-scale movements on the wall behind him were in reality tiny little dustpan-and-cardboard movements on the bright screen in front of him. The light from the projector glowed from below onto the rapt face of a Messiah, revealing to his disciples how the revolution would unfold. I didn't believe in God, but, for a while there, I think I believed in Claude.

No Confrontations

Not believing in God didn't seem any impediment to my progress through the parochial church hierarchy. By the age of sixteen, I was not only a regular Master of Ceremonies but also the Under-Sacristan. I'm not sure if that was my real title, but I know that Stephen Fairbrother was St Laurence's nominal Sacristan, while I seemed to do most of the actual work. A Sacristan looks after the contents of the Sacristy, which – excluding the Rev, who could just about look after himself – comprised all the trinkets of a ceremonial religion. I was in charge of the holy bread and the holy wine – yes, even the body and blood of Christ need stock control – and had to make sure before every service that the Rev's amazing technicolour dreamcoats, in the form of his alb, his chasuble and his other paraphernalia, were correctly selected for that particular day: red for a bog-standard Sunday, purple for Maundy Thursday, gold for Easter Day etc. They all had to be folded according to an exact pattern which the Rev imparted to me early in my career and which, of course, I am totally forbidden to reveal to you, lest you sinners begin to fold your pyjamas that way and thereby gain unfair access to Heaven.

Being a trusted Under-Sacristan, I had a set of keys to the church, which meant I was also given the dubious honour of being the sole server at one of the weekday Matins services. Every Wednesday morning for two years I would get up at seven o'clock to trudge through half a mile of drizzle and darkness, unlock the church, switch on all the lights, shiver through to the sacristy, don my black cassock, select and fold the Rev's weekday costume, pour three mouthfuls of white wine into the chalice, transfer three white wafers to the silver salver, mumble "Good morning, father" to the Rev (who wasn't my father) while helping him on with his dreamcoats, lead him through to the Lady Chapel, run through a ridiculous 30-minute rigmarole in the exclusive company of the Rev and an old lady who always sat in the front pew at 7:59, eat my wafer, gulp my wine, lead the Rev back to the sacristy, help him off with his dreamcoats, put them away, whip off my cassock, stumble out into the awakening Market Place, and trudge off again through the drizzle and gloom to school.

I think it fair to say that 'irksome' is a rather mild word for this time-wasting crap. At the age of eighteen, the week before I finally escaped from Long Eaton to the seaside, I did the Wednesday Matins stint for the last time, did my drill in Claude's Army on Sunday morning for the last time, handed in my keys, said goodbye to the Rev, Claude and the choir, accepted the invitation to turn up again at St Laurence's whenever I came back, and then went home to write a letter to the Rev (cc Claude) telling them that I never believed all that Christian rot, that they wouldn't be seeing me again, and that I wished them all the worst of luck. At the time I didn't fancy confrontations.

I never received a reply. And, weddings and funerals apart, I have never set foot in a church of any description from that day to this. Nor shall I. They're all mad.

4

Life on the Outside

"None, Actually, Sir"

Now here's a funny thing. If I understand it right, education is supposed to prepare you for something. Whether that something is a job, a university or just life seems to be a point of debate, but something after you leave school anyway. So it seems a little strange that, until the very last week before my escape from LEGS, no-one there had asked me what I was going to do after school. There was no careers advice, no prompting to pursue any particular subject, no suggestions of universities to apply for, nothing Zip nada, zilch. Not so much funny, perhaps, as incompetent.

At the time, though, this 'backwardness in coming forwards'[30] on the part of Old Man Grimes and his cohorts played right into my hands, since I had an unfortunate tendency to go along with whatever people suggested I do – a potentially fatal human attribute of which I would encourage youngsters to divest themselves at the earliest opportunity. I suspect they all assumed that I, like everyone else around me, would apply to university. Well, I had no intention of doing so and even now can recall the juvenile glee with which I replied to my French teacher's casual query in the Upper VI (Arts) Room:

"And which universities have *you* applied to, Guise?"

"None, actually, sir."

---

[30] "Now, don't be backwards in coming forwards" was one of our headmaster's favourite phrases, as it were. And that was the other one: morning assembly was made bearable by the lively betting on how many times he would say "as it were" during his morning 'notices'. Goodness, how long, long ago those days now seem

The irony is that it was my loss, as revealed in the Half Crown public house six months later.

So, one balmy noontime in June 1969, aged 17 and with a buzzing, vacant space between my ears, I walked out of the gymnasium where I'd sat my last A-Level exam (Geography Paper II, as I recall), picked up my bag, floated through the double-doors and straight out of the LEGS yard with my 13 years of schooldays finally, gloriously, miraculously behind me.

What I was going to do next I had no idea. Well, actually, I was going to watch man land on the Moon live on the telly, which just about knocked everything that had happened in the previous 17 years into a cocked space helmet, but I mean after that. What I didn't realize then, and what some people, alas, never realize at all, is that it's actually possible to earn a living doing something you enjoy. Difficult maybe, if all you enjoy is loafing in front of the telly – but after all, TV critics are human beings too. As for me, I enjoyed travelling (not that I'd done much), writing (ditto), reading, cycling, buying records... activities I now know to be positively awash with career prospects.

However, back in 1969 my dull little brain, beaten even duller and littler by 17 years of conformity, could come up with only two options:

- working in a shop (because midad did)
- working in a bank (because my cousin did).

What narrow strand the young man sees, 'twixt endless swamp and boundless seas! Sorry, came over all poetic there – I promise it won't happen again.

The bank sounded as though it might be the more lucrative and so it was that I got hold of an application form for the Westminster Bank, filled it in, asked midad to buy me a dark-green suit from Heard's on Derby Road, attended an interview in Sheffield (of which the only thing I can remember is being unable to re-fold the broadsheet newspaper I'd foolishly picked up in the waiting room) and got the job. I think the suit did the trick.

And so on Monday 25th August 1969, my short days of freedom drew to an abrupt close. Well, no, that's unfair on the Westminster Bank in Derby, which itself represented freedom of a kind. Freely I cycled to catch the 7·43 from Sawley Junction every morning; freely and luxuriously I lunched on sausage and chips at Betty's Café[31] on London Road and freely I railed and cycled home again. What's more, I was actually paid: to the melodious tune of £32 16s 8d per month[32], which was enough to invest in LPs more regularly than just every Beatles release, of which, alas, there were but two more to come.

In between the sausages and the *Motown Chartbusters (Volume III)*, there was some bank work of course, of which you'll be relieved to learn I shall not overburden you. Retrospectively noteworthy, though, is that the year 1969 stood precariously on the cusp of the computer revolution and I was lucky (as I now recognize) to have a very brief experience of pre-computer office life.

From his raised and glass-fronted cubicle set back from the main well of the front office, Mr Coxon, the branch's Chief Clerk, surveyed a scene that would not have looked out of place fifty years before. Besuited young men and beskirted young women sat beneath the high, ornate ceiling at sturdy desks, where we pored with a mostly silent intensity over files and typed letters. Usually to the right, but occasionally to the left of each clerk's work area, lay several sheets of scrap paper bearing the black, blue and red scribbles that were our calculations for the day and which we were obliged to retain for checking in case of a discrepency in the end-of-day balance. No screen was to be seen.

As the Junior, one of my own jobs was to register the day's Savings and Deposits transactions and, yes, this was done in two heavy ledgers, eighteen inches long and several inches thick. I was rather disappointed to be given a biro for this, as my entries – though neat as time allowed – looked rather cheap and nasty compared with the earlier columns of inked entries. Mine, each duly initialled "RGG" must have been among the last ever entries in these old books, as the foot-soldiers of Mr Wilson's white-hot technology army had in fact already breached the walls of the Westminster Bank...

---

[31] Now the Café Loco. The bank is now the office of a philatelic auction business. Of all things.

[32] Which, strangely, was to be exactly my *hourly* rate 30 years later. Spooky or what? What, probably.

The Long-Running Affair, Episode 1

It was square, it was blue and it was big — too big in fact for the Westminster Bank, Midland Road branch, and so the IBM mainframe lived at their Irongate branch. This, however, didn't stop us from having a 'machine room'. (What a great phrase that is, summing up neatly that era when the computer 'machines', like caged tigers, were best kept in a separate room.)

Being a little too green to be allowed in front of the customers, I spent my first few months bashing the branch's current-account transactions into a data-entry machine in this back room. We had no VDU, of course; what I typed in was displayed not on a screen, but on a roll of paper that chugged out of the machine like *Grandstand*'s teleprinter:

```
Aston Villa 4
Mrs Grimethorpe (Shopping A/c) 0
```

And no disk for data transfer either, nor even punched cards – and no, not even magnetic tape. Any more guesses? In fact, with every beat of the keyboard, what lurched out of the left-hand side of the machine was yard after yard of very yellow, very fragile *paper* tape. Paper tape with a crude pattern of holes in it, holes that represented of course Mrs Grimethorpe's cheque for 2/6 or the Carriage & Wagon Works' wage bill for £46,019. 4s. 8d.

Hundreds, if not thousands, of transactions passed through the branch each day and it was mind-numbing work, I can tell you. Fortunately, as you will have gathered, my particular mind was already pretty numb and my mistakes were few and far between. However, corrections naturally had to be made, or else Mrs G would end up paying British Railways' weekly wages. It was very simple really. If you entered an erroneous transaction, you crossed it through on the printout and tore it out of the tape. Yes, as in fingers or scissors – and of course sellotape to join the two pieces of punched tape back together again. I swear I'm not making this up! The efficacy of the British banking sector of 1969 did indeed depend on the ability of me – and hundreds like me up and down the country – to interpret a series of holes on a paper tape and repair them with the old sticky-back plastic. *Blue Peter* would have been proud of us.

And the surreal, Heath-Robinsonesque images don't end there. Oh, no. At the end of the day, as I'm sure you wizened old computer folk will know, our branch's batch of data had to be whizzed by some fiendish means to the Big Blue at Irongate. And the fiendish means in 1969 was for yours truly to assemble neatly the reels of paper tape in a little brown suitcase, slip out of the side door onto London Road, ride the Derby Corporation bus into town, with my little brown bag of data neatly perched on my besuited and often besweated little lap, and present myself at Irongate, Derby's main Westminster Bank branch, where I joined the queue of other data-laden boys and girls from the suburbs.

When my turn came, I'd approach Big Blue, feed my first little paper loop onto a big reel that could have been, indeed probably was, featured in the background of *Dr Strangelove*, and then type in my secret digits. If Big Blue liked my digits, He gave me a whirr of approval and there followed a very tense few minutes during which I , along with those impatient suburbanites in the queue behind me, watched the reel spin into a frenzy and prayed that Big Blue's dreaded Big Bell wouldn't alert us, the rest of the branch and much of central Derby to that *bête noir* of the data entry clerk: a syntax error. Yes, if He found any little thing amiss – a missing account number or a slip of sellotape carelessly placed over a hole – the giant bell on Big Blue's side, which was rather like those that signal the next round of a boxing match, would sound through that great hall[33], telling staff and customers alike that the youth biting his nails by the Big Machine had made a Big Mistake.

Oh, how I dreaded that bell! How frantically I pulled off the reel to do my emergency tearing and taping! How my dark-green suit darkened even more with my adolescent sweat!

In fact my time in the bank saw a number of embarrassments, only one more of which am I prepared to share with you now. Eventually I had been allowed to present myself in front of humans rather than machines and one lunchtime the queue at my till lay five deep, so that the young, uniformed policeman had been waiting some time before standing in front of me.

"You rang?", he said.

"I beg your pardon?"

---

[33] Which is still there, incidentally, as the main bar of J D Wetherspoon's *The Standing Order*

"You rang the alarm, sir. Can I be of assistance?"

I'm not sure I'd been called 'sir' before and so became a little flustered. After some debate, and some anxious watch-glancing in my queue, we established that it had been so long since I'd been shown where the secret, silent alarm was that I'd been tapping it with my foot for some time to the rhythm of *I Heard It Through the Grapevine*. And so disciplined were Britain's policemen that P C Grommett had actually queued for ten minutes before his turn came around to attend the emergency! I'm not sure whether the incident reassured me or not.

Another Modicum Moment

Thus was the bank's daily drill: nothing if not incident-packed, but possibly not with the sort of incidents I wanted to endure for another 48 years.

'Possibly' turned to 'definitely' when, one Friday night, I met up with some erstwhile LEGS chums for a beer at the newly opened Half Crown on Nottingham Road, Long Eaton. This epoch-making event – well, for me at least – was actually my first time in a pub (I was still under-age and, then as now, law-abiding by default), which I showed by ordering the first thing I saw behind the bar: a pint of Swan Vesta. No, just kidding. I ordered a pint of bitter and proceeded to spend the rest of the evening trying to down the foul-tasting brew. This assault on my taste buds, however, was as nothing compared to the enticing assault on my eyes and ears.

My friends, most of whom I'd never seen out of school uniform, presented a bewitchingly trendy, late-60s appearance: shaggy hair, sweaty sweaters and chins proudly decked out with beard fluff. Some of the chaps looked a bit rough too. Moreover, their easy chat of tiddlywinks clubs and debating societies, nine o'clock seminars and ten o'clock tutorials left me spellbound, the more so as I hadn't a clue what seminars and tutorials were. As I sat in the corner on the red Draylon bench, with my neat Westminster-Bank hair, straight-ribbed, roll-neck jumper and clinging Crimplene slacks, my future seemed suddenly to present some options. Yes, another 'modicum of control' moment.

The next day I bounded up the old 'Pax-Lux' steps to pore over Long Eaton Library's copies of university prospectuses; within a week I'd applied to six courses; and within a month got a late, late place at the

University College of Wales in Aberystwyth, starting the following Autumn. With no interview deemed necessary, I hadn't even been to Aberystwyth and certainly couldn't pronounce it.

Goodness knows what midad thought. One minute I was contributing to the household income, the next I was a long-term liability. If only children thought like that at the time.

The Furthest Place from Anywhere [Red Word]

Radio presenter John Peel has said that wherever you start from in Britain, Aberystwyth is always the furthest place away. Aber couldn't have been a bigger contrast to Long Eaton if it had been on the Moon. Where LE had a grimy canal, Aber had the open sea; where LE had no view further than a hundred yards, Aber had hills and headlands that drew your breath; where everyone in LE spoke with an Erewash Valley accent, some people in Aber didn't even speak English. Miraculous!

The biggest shock to the system, though, was that old impostor: social class. I thought I was working class, and had no problem with that; I knew the middle class existed, and had no problem with that either. But never having actually met them before, at least not *en masse*, I was overwhelmed by the bourgeoisie who, in Aber, were just everywhere: doctors' sons, professors' daughters, monarchists, rugby players, ballroom dancers, youths with cars, people who said 'barth', girls who said 'oh lovely', boys who wore bow-ties and played violins. Mesmerized, I reacted by retreating into my shell and prioritizing work before all else, since in the lectures, libraries and essays was a structure I could relate to and where I could, with a little hard work, forge a slot where I felt secure.

As the first year progressed, I was fortunate to fall in with a crowd who made me feel included and most of whom – another miracle – I still meet up with on a regular basis over 30 years later. One Sunday afternoon, however, while we were indulging in Cardiganshire's preferred recreational drug of the 1970s – tea – I discovered that, middle-class or not, they all shared the same shortcoming: not one of them knew that Tuesday is green.

Nor that Wednesday is yellow, August red and Gareth Edwards brown and blue. Not only did they fail to perceive words in colour, but they also failed to see any letters in colour; nor any numbers. Further interrogation [white word] even revealed a bewildering tendency on their part to see a sequence of numbers as simply a vertical column; of letters as just a horizontal line; of the months of the year as just, well, monochrome words with no spatial properties whatsoever.

Subsequent research in several countries [metallic grey word] on several continents [ditto] has found this general failing to be not only widespread but – how can I put it? – virtually universal! (How close I may have been during this research to being quietly escorted away to a nearby white van I'm not sure.)

Now I'm certain that some of you reading this otherwise rational ramble [both red words] must also have attended Brooklands Infants and Junior School in Long Eaton, and now is your chance to reassure me that these colourful, three-dimensional images I have of all textual and numeric information are simply the result of how we were taught spelling and arithmetic in the 1950s and early '60s... rather than the chronic effects of an unhappy accident in the Dulux paint factory which I have otherwise managed to erase from my memory. Weren't both the alphabet and our 'times tables' up there on the wall behind Mr Pyefinch's[34] left ear in Class 4? And weren't they in colour?

'Tuesday' is indupitably green, isn't it? Isn't it?? An e-mail will do: richard_guise@yahoo.com

Strange and Frigid Brew

Despite my own harmless version of weirdness, the initial sensation at Aberystwyth of having fallen into a fantastic world of alien beings never really left me and this was at its sharpest during the Carpenter Hall 'initiation ceremony'.

We victims (all the hall's freshers) were told to line up after dinner[35] on the cafeteria stairs wearing just our swimming trunks. One by one those ahead of me were led around the corner to the back yard, from where, presently, screams, splashes and "Yeaarrrrgh!!!!!"'s rent the chill November air. My turn round the corner revealed a tin bath full of what looked like yesterday's leftovers mixed with used engine oil

---

[34] Real name [... and greeny-blue].

[35] Somewhere between Sawley Junction and Aberystwyth, 'dinner' had switched from a midday to an evening meal. I suspect this may have taken place at Dovey Junction, which has that air of cultural transformation.

and salad cream. I subsequently discovered it was actually mayonnaise, but otherwise I was spot on.

Having been totally (totally) immersed in the frigid brew, we were led, still barefoot and surely looking like the survivors of a sixteenth-century culinary eruption in Franz-Josef Land, to the pebble beach opposite, where it was made gleefully clear to us that the hall's showers would be out of bounds to freshers until at least 11 p.m. and that the lurching black rollers of the Arctic Ocean (known thereabouts as the Irish Sea) constituted our only hope of toiletry improvement until after the next indignity. Already frozen to – and beyond – the bone, I joined my miserable colleagues in the breakers. Thankfully, my memory cells must have been frozen by the shock, as I have no further recollections until surfacing, as directed, in the lower Marine Bar with a pint of Worthington E in front of me.

There was some game. I think it required an intimate knowledge of either the Llanelli front row or Tom and Jerry or Vivaldi's *Four Seasons* (rum folk, these Welsh). My general knowledge was found wanting and I found myself coerced into drinking several pints of 'E' down in one, having previously managed only half a pint down in 30 minutes. The number 11 seems to echo through the years, but 11 pints would surely have seen me out for the count until about 1976. Whatever, I was ill, I was filthy, I was apparently initiated and I was thereafter on constant alert for subsequent attacks from the *Forciau Outerspaciau Cymraeg* (the Alien Forces of Wales).

You may be surprised to learn, however, that I very much enjoyed the Aber experience and didn't doubt for a single day, a single moment even, that university was a better option than the bank, i.e. than real life. To have fallen into the generation that escaped National Service at one end and student loans at the other was a wonderful thing. To be able to study for free a pointless but fascinating subject was another.

All of which makes the concept of a student strike even more difficult to comprehend. "And whom", as someone pithily asked at the time, "will that inconvenience?" No-one but ourselves of course, and so, since I disapproved then as now of the very concept of a strike, even if you're doing something useful, I simply worked on, harder than ever. While the Trotskyists and Jenkinsists were occupying the Student's Union, I was occupying the Llandinam Library with even more regularity, and by candlelight to boot – the power-workers' strike having done for the electricity. I don't think there were actually picket lines, but I would have happily crossed one if I could have found it, as I've managed to subsequently. While most of my other political views have veered further and further to the 'left' with age, my angle on strikes has stayed steadfastly on the 'right'. Shows how ridiculous this 'left' and 'right' thing is, doesn't it?

So I studied something full-time for three years. What it actually was escapes me for the moment, and whether I've been called upon to use any of the knowledge thus gained is likewise unclear. I'm pretty sure it involved some sort of maps, an ancient desert city called Mohenjo Daro, a fair sprinkling of statistics and bucketfuls of logarithms. It certainly involved my first-ever encounter with a calculator.

The Long-Running Affair, Episode 2

Now, when you read the word 'calculator' just then, those of you born after 1960 probably pictured something rectangular and flat, with little numbers in a little screen, right?. Maybe the 1955 generation pictured something angled towards you with finger-sized keys, chunky green numbers and a reassuring, plastic-type click. Er, did anyone picture a heavy, black cylinder with concentric slots in the top? No? Well, it must have been just the thirty of us that met in Aber's Geography lab for a few strange Mondays in 1972, then. (Ah yes, Geography, that must have been it.)

At a cost of £90 we were given one each and our lecturer Dr Williams made sure we knew how much Mr Heath's government had invested in us. The purpose of the cylinders was to help us calculate r. I'm not sure I ever grasped what r actually was, although I'm pretty confident it was a close relation to Miss Bottom's x. You moved some of the coloured tabs around the slots at the top, which made a kind of whirring sound, then you moved some more, then you flipped some kind of switch and a number appeared in a window on the bottom of the cylinder, a number comprising rolling digits not unlike a car's odometer. This was r. And r was, er, something to do with the distribution of black people in Chicago. No, it was the probability of being dead in Llanfihangel, wasn't it? No, give me a minute, yes, I'm sure it was the number of apples in a pie chart. Well, perhaps not. Anyway, it was definitely r and that, beyond a shadow of a doubt was what Dr Williams wanted.

Pretty soon, however, my magic cylinder started to grind when it should have whirred, its little coloured tabs began to resist movement and I was relegated once again to my faithful log tables. Additionally, however, we were allowed one tantalizing, but brief, encounter with the department's own Big Blue.

I'm only guessing it was an IBM, but all the clues were there: it lived in a locked room of its own, we were never allowed to see it and we had to book two weeks in advance even to communicate with it. Well, 'communicate' is rather an exaggeration, for in my pre-booked ten-minute slot, I simply typed the prescribed code into the old 'Grandstand' teleprinter...

```
if <this> then <that>
print <that>
rem what about the 2:15 at haydock park?
```

duly saw my effort clattered back to me on the old toilet roll, pressed a big black key and tore off my section of toilet roll before giving up my seat to the next human cog in the machine. Paper-clipping my piece of curly toilet paper to a page of neatly written calculations took me half a percentage point nearer an honours degree. The purpose of the little program, of course, was to calculate r.

I don't know what Dr Williams did with his r's, and I'm not sure I want to.

11. Derby Midland Railway Station before the latest crop of vandals in charge of Britain's railways demolished its façade in favour of a square brick-and-glass box. Arriving here was an exciting start to every working day in 1969 (about ten years before this photo). *Photo: author*

5

Geographer at Large

Reality and Other Distractions

Now, Geography's only use to humanity, of course, is to give Geography teachers some material to teach in Geography classes, where the ablest pupils will be inspired enough to go on to learn more Geography at university, enabling *them* to teach it in their turn in yet more Geography classes. The only missing skill here is how to teach. There therefore exist other university departments where ex-Geography teachers teach would-be Geography teachers how to teach other would-be Geography teachers Geography.

I signed up with one of these departments at Nottingham University and spent the next year in yet more intimate contact with this interesting but mostly harmless breed of human, that lives and breathes maps, except when it's living and breathing pie charts, and searches all corners of this wide and diverse planet for the fascinating yet elusive *r*.

In case you think I'm being unfairly brisk in my assessment of a Geographer's skills, let me whisk you briefly some 20 years forward to 1995, to a rural Spanish summer on a railway station called Vilajuiga. Here, two friends had arranged to meet and take a pleasant and much-planned stroll in the countryside. Jim and I had both come sensibly equipped with walking boots, walking sticks, compasses and large-scale maps, encased of course in regulation plastic Geographers' map-cases, for we were both regulation plastic Geographers[36]. Indeed, I'd been studying the map for some time on

---

[36] Rather like being HIV-positive, being a Geographer is something you always are, regardless of your subsequent life.

the platform before Jim arrived. After a brief but enthusiastic greeting, we set off westwards and within one minute – óne minute! – of our stepping off the end of the platform, we were completely lost. More than this, we were lost in the middle of a vast area of giant bamboo, with several unexpected paths veering off at jaunty angles, and had somehow contrived to lose eye contact with each other. And this was, I swear, within fifty metres of our departure point. This is but one example of **The Geographer's Law of Reality**, which states:

> *Where map and reality diverge, it is always reality that is at fault.*

Back in 1974, you may be wondering what had driven me back to the classroom after having left it so willingly just four years before. Such a thought also crossed my own befuddled mind about a thousand times over the following months – indeed still does, and yet I can come up with no other cause than a subconscious desire for revenge.

I was a very poor teacher. Correction: I was a very poor *policeman*, for this was the essence of the job both in the run-down Nottinghamshire mining village where I did my teaching practice and in the sleepy Cotswold market town where I attempted the real thing. Children of all ages wandered freely about my classes, causing minor but persistent mayhem, while I found myself unable to stop them, being consistently puzzled that the opportunity to discover the reason for the Atacama Desert's existence did not guarantee their rapt attention. The 'modicum moment' arrived briskly this time: I handed my notice in after just three weeks. There being a mysterious lack of local contenders for the spare title of Assistant Geography Teacher, I was persuaded to stay for a year however.

It was a nightmare. Literally. The blank white fear of facing an unruly class of farmers' offspring with no lesson prepared is still occasionally drawn from the depths at 3:30 a.m. to bring me bolt upright and grasping a sweat-stained sheet. It wasn't just their unruly behaviour that frustrated me, nor even their disinterest in the Atacama Desert, but in many cases I'm afraid it was their simple, rank stupidity. I remember one boy – let's call him Tom – who seemed unable to bring back to school any of the books or files he'd taken home the previous evening.

"Have you done your homework, Tom?"

"Yesur, but oi forgot moy foil."

"Now there's a surprise."

"Nosur, oy always forgets it."

(The arrows of sarcasm, which had so regularly struck home when aimed at me as a LEGS pupil, flew way over Tom's head.) Then one day, miraculously, Tom arrived in the Geography room with a green file clenched in his substantial fist.

"Looksur, oi've remembered moy foil!"

"Well done, Tom."

Tom proudly took his place by the window, through which, within one minute of my introduction to the fascinating world of glacial erosion, he had managed to eject his file. We were on the first floor.

"Moy foil's garn through the window, sur!"

"On its own, Tom?"

"No, moy ruler's garn out thur too!"

"Well, you'd better go down and fetch them, Tom. Don't be long."

At which invitation, Tom proceeded to clamber through the first-floor window. I'm not making this up. Having physically hauled him back from the brink, I indicated the stairwell. Now, this wasn't one of Tom's jokes, since he had none. His belongings had 'garn through' the window and so, to retrieve them, he planned to do likewise. Even now I don't know why I waited as long as three weeks to resign.

However, I've tried to carry forward something positive from every workplace and that Cotswold school gave me a vital baseline to be recalled whenever I begin to find any activity tedious or annoying: *at least this isn't as bad as teaching.*

It also taught me a neat trick which I'm pleased to share with any unfortunate teachers amongst you. Physical attacks on unruly pupils were, alas, outlawed even in my day. However, there exists the following simple method of inflicting pain on a persistent offender without either physical contact or use of the old flying board-rubber.

1.   Bring said offender to the front of the class and stand him with his back flat against the blackboard (if such a device still exists).

2.   Instruct him to stand still and silent for five minutes.

3. Continue with the lesson as normal.

4. Every time you saunter within three feet of your victim make a small but sudden lurch in his direction. You can guarantee that the obnoxious head of the obnoxious villain will jerk back with a sharp crack against the board.

"Ouch!"

"Try and stand still, Jenkins, will you? And silent means silent."

The Road to the Aisles

My second escape from the black pit of the classroom was even sweeter than the first, and the more so as, belatedly becoming a little streetwise, I'd set out to find a job I might actually be good at and might – it was surely possible – might just enjoy.

In the 1970s, Pink Stamps were a rather poor competitor to the ubiquitous Green Shield Stamps, except oddly enough on the Isle of Wight. Customers at certain supermarkets and petrol stations received with each purchase little pink stamps, which they stuck in little pink books, with which they bought little pink gifts from little pink catalogues. My job was to deliver to the outlets the little pink books and little pink catalogues, in a little pink van that announced boldly on its side: 'Gifts for Everyone'.

As Green Shield dominated the market, these outlets were few and far between (except on the Isle of Wight). Being a northener in Pink Stamps' eyes, I was allocated 'The Midlands and the North', a vast territory stretching from Holyhead to Felixstowe and from Potter's Bar to Inverness, most of which I had to cover every fortnight. I thus rarely saw my boss and spent almost all day every day on the road and on expenses. After the dark disciplines of the bank and the school, words cannot express how wonderful this experience was. Let me try, though: brilliant, fantastic, stupendous! Nope, these words don't quite do the trick. What about…

Yeeeeeeeea aaaarrrrraaa waaahhoooo ooooooooo!!!!

Yes, that goes some way towards it.

Driving that Leyland Sherpa was the best job I ever did, and I don't know why I ever gave it up. Ah yes, I do – the firm went bust. While it lasted, however, I spent day after glorious day on the open road, with just my maps, my casette recorder and my thermos flask for company. As anyone who's left a grinding job will know, everything you do for the first few weeks is done with that extra inner glow that comes from knowing your erstwhile colleagues are at that very moment still slogging away in the pit. Some days I'd get on the road way before dawn just so as to be sipping my mid-morning coffee on the promenade at Llandudno or by the docks at Lowestoft, in the knowledge that, 200 miles away, some sorry Geography teacher was facing the 26 blank faces of 3R and realizing what the R stood for.

I still did a bit of Geology for fun. The van schedule was flexible enough to give me an hour or two to hammer around in the carboniferous limestone of North Yorkshire or the hornblende schist of Anglesey. When the van was stolen in Crouch End, my boss wasn't surprised at the Mahler cassettes (2) and Moody Blues cassettes (3) listed under 'Personal items', but did query the geological hammer (1) and ammonites (24).

Driving two or three hundred miles a day for months on end also gave me time to think. Tricky chap, thought. Among the many Easy Solutions to the World's Problems that emerged from the endless M6 northbound was...

How to Educate the Masses Without Riots and Suicides

Let's begin at the beginning: what's this education thing for? Well, you're born, you live a bit and then you die. During the 'live a bit' bit, your basic requirements are a regular supply of Marmite, a serviceable hat and some time in the sun. Since only one of these comes free (or, if you're unfortunate enough to live in Middlesbrough, none), you'll need to earn some money. OK, it's true that some people manage to cadge off others for most of their lives, but this still leaves the cadgees needing to pay their way. So you need a job, or almost certainly several jobs, and they require skills. You also need the ability just to deal with life things – things such as reading a bus timetable, driving a car, cooking pasta and knowing your hat size. (I'd got this far by about Warrington.)

So there's a bunch of subjects that everyone needs to learn; you know the list: reading, writing, filling in a tax form, changing a wheel and so on . Since the days when I figured this out in the old Pink Stamps van, new basic skills have turned up (mouse-clicking, video-setting) while others have become redundant (double-declutching, Tippexing). But even then I couldn't help noticing how different the list was from the school curriculum I'd so recently been required to follow as both pupil and teacher. There was a whole raft of stuff that people, notably small people, spent days and days learning, but which were Probably Unnecessary For Most Ordinary Purposes. PUFMOP stuff: History, Geography, Latin, Art, Games; triangles, pulleys, Battles of Crécy, the rules of Rugby Union... all there on the timetable, but all indubitably PUFMOP stuff. Could there be some other purpose of education?

Well OK, guys, I admit it: there's such a thing as knowledge. Mankind's been beavering away in all sorts of back rooms for centuries and centuries, building up this knowledge thing and it would be reckless indeed not to pass it on (although in the case of Rugby Union I would make an exception). How would it look if, with every generation, about 20,000 of the smarter types invented the wheel again? It wouldn't take them long, of course, what with trains and Toyotas whooshing past on something that assumed a certain familiar shape every time they stopped, but all the same it would be something of a time-waster. But, hold on just one minute. Does *everyone* have to learn about the wheel, about axle-loading, friction coefficients and material science? Wouldn't there be enough folks actually *interested* in that kind of stuff to ensure mankind as a species didn't forget? I suggest there might. (There's Preston.)

Likewise, what's the actual point, the actual benefit to the Earth and its peoples, of every one of 40,000,000 British schoolchildren between 1950 and 1990 knowing the French tactics at the Battle of Crécy? Wouldn't just fifty do? Or five? There are such things as books after all, which are, I've found, a jolly useful repository for things you suddenly need to know at 3:30 a.m. Children's brains are, I suggest, a rather inefficient and unreliable platform for data storage.

So essential subjects – the skills – are for everyone, but the PUFMOP subjects are just for those who are interested. No disinterested pupils, then – could this be possible? This seemed, and still does seem, like some kind of a breakthrough in the old education game.

Another is the way I reckoned it should be done. (Isn't that the University of Lancaster?) It's easy really. At birth, everyone's given a fixed number of 'education vouchers' which you can spend whenever you want on whatever subjects you want, so long as you spend enough on the essential skills subjects before you start using them up on PUFMOP subjects. Up to age 14 or so, your parents spend the vouchers for you. Thereafter, you can spend your remaining vouchers immediately if you want, and all of them on eight years' full-time study of Greek mythology if you really want, and for all anyone else cares. Alternatively, you may want to go straight to that motorbike workshop just off the High Street, earn some dosh, leave home, hitch your way to the Atacama Desert, wonder why it's there, get involved with a local Indian girl, raise three children, only one of whom is named Bernard, bring them back to Nottingham, discover with dismay that the old market has gone but with joy that your education vouchers are still in the sideboard drawer, and then – *only then* – invest some of them in Geography evening classes at The People's College, there to discover with interest – *with interest*, Jenkins! – the significance of offshore currents to the peculiar climate of northern Chile. And no-one else will care if you do. It's called choice and it's the solution to both the discipline and the resource problems in schools.

I wonder if anyone else knows?

(Here's Carlisle – time for a break.)

When Pink Stamps went under I took a job with a road haulage company, getting hold of part-loads that would profitably fill a container going to Esbjerg, or Gothenburg or Helsinki and all points north. This job, which was called freight forwarding, was another one of those which, had I any gumption, I would have realized existed before I drifted into the black pit of teaching; but which, it appears, no-one in education had heard of.

I won't test your powers of endurance by attempting to dress up the haulage business with jolly anecdotes of gammy groupage or dodgy dunnage – other than to remark in passing that all its technical terms happen to end in -age, pronounced -idge. That's about it really.

After two years, having felt the need to cash in a few more education vouchers and having signed up for a full-time course in Transport (for they exist), a strange thing happened. Just as I was scratching around trying to piece together enough from my meagre savings to pay for the course, the grey phone rang on my freight forwarder's desk.

"Cause on grey here." (This was the year of Reginald Perrin.)

A gruff-voice at the other end said he was sorry to disturb me, but he'd heard that I was about to undertake a year's study and wondered if I would do him the favour of accepting £7,000 tax-free from his firm to support me through the year, no strings attached? I remember my eyes opening unfeasibly wide and my mouth suddenly forming an internal layer of sand-paper, as I tried to form the two words that together seemed an appropriate response:

"Y...ng..ng.. ye.. yesss, pl...l...please!"

Before I left the haulage firm, though, the transport manager did me the great favour of arranging a lift aboard one of his vehicles travelling the regular route from Nottinghamshire to the South of France. For free! (Do you occasionally have a short period when everything goes inexplicably and unnaturally right? Yes, short, aren't they?)

The two-day trip to Paris with Bill was OK, but eventually you do tend to run out of things to talk about with anyone, even when you share a passing interest in mobile lifting equipment. At the transshipment depot in the northern suburbs of Paris, I took the opportunity of a paperwork delay to say my *adieus* to the long-suffering Bill and set out for the south under my own steam. I was 26 and had never been abroad alone before, nor indeed to France at all. It was exhilarating.

The Métro, the Gare de Lyon, the sleek grey coaches of the Corail train (predecessor of the TGV); the black-and-white photographs of the Côte d'Azur in the compartments, the monosyllabic French conversations in the corridor; the strangely elegant houses, the startlingly wide rivers, the hypnotic first view of the blue, blue Mediterranean; and eventually, the first seductive caress of that soft southern air on my skin as I stepped down from the train at Menton. I was more alive than I thought possible, and wondered helplessly why I hadn't done this before. (But I've been doing it ever since. Travelling, I mean.)

As a newly poverty-stricken student (the cheque hadn't yet arrived), my plan was to travel the length and breadth of France by train, staying in *auberges de jeunesse*, although I'd never stayed in youth hostels in England before – or since, in fact. I thought I'd start at the bottom-right and therefore Menton was the first, and possibly best, stopover. It was here that other exotic 'firsts' came tumbling one after the other into my previously plain vanilla life. First bunk (a bit claustrophobic), first ground coffee (a different drink entirely), first Mediterranean beach (crowded), complete with first topless female bather (pert), first tentative paddle in warm, transparent seawater (unforgettably pleasurable), first water I could float in (novel), first meal ordered in a foreign language (such a triumph that I repeated the same meal in the same café the following day), first rat (just looked like a big mouse)... generally first class all round.

One surprise was that the French did not, even in 1978, use the past historic tense so central to the A-level curriculum at Long Eaton Grammar School. I know this because my carefully sculpted question *"Est-ce qu'il fût le train que j'aurais dû prendre?"* was met by the railway employee at Tours with a mixture of suppressed sniggering and incipient fear that's difficult to forget. I think an English equivalent might be "Alack, but wouldst say, fellow, that my waggon is thrice passed?" Less surprising was that the French vocabulary required to change trains, buy street maps and check in at youth hostels in France (i.e. that required by late twentieth-century Englishmen abroad) is not that found in 17th-century texts examining the twin themes of *l'honneur des gentilhommes* and *la gloire de la France.* I rest my case. On *Voie Un.*

Despite my occasional communication problems, though, I did manage to cover most of the French rail network – twice, if I recall – in three weeks of blissfully random travel. In one of those little time-space tricks that life plays on us, my wanderings included just half an hour sitting on a bench in Grenoble, admiring the same twinkling Alpine peaks that I was later to stare at more or less every evening for three years, from a riverside flat less than a mile away, where I discovered they were the peaks of Chamrousse.

12. Menton, Cote d'Azur, where the water was a fraction warmer than in the Grange Park Tortures of the 1960s. August 1978. *Photo: author*

6

Putting the Sport in Transport

The Lonely, Slowly Spinning Room

Now, where do you think mini-roundabouts come from? A mini-roundabout tree, perhaps? The droppings of the fabulous mini-roundabout bird of Western Samoa? No? Well, let me tell you. They come from the desks of mini-roundabout engineers, who skulk in the depths of County Halls all over Britain, with nothing but a Mars Bar and a Transport degree for sustenance.

For mini-roundabouts – their history, design and benefits – are but one of the many fascinating and practical topics that you learn about in a Transport degree course, such as the one I took at Cranfield, which is – as its promotional literature so accurately announced – "50 miles from anywhere". (In fact, it's just beyond the southbound caff at Newport Pagnell service station.) How far one metro train should be behind the other; why trolley buses are sometimes better than both ordinary buses *and* trams; what value the Department of Transport puts on a life potentially saved by a new set of traffic lights (£15,000 at the time of asking); on a limb potentially not severed (something rather less). Oh, there's no end to it. Frankly, I was very impressed by the whole thing, and especially the subsidized bars.

1978/9 was a very severe winter and one lunchtime several friends and I found ourselves observing the ever-deepening snow in the car park outside Mitchell Hall bar. (We were observing it from *inside* Mitchell Hall bar, naturally.) Our Mass Transit lecturer happened to be present, in fact happened to be leaning in very close proximity to the Ruddles hand-pump, and took an early and wise decision to cancel the afternoon's academic events. What he actually said, I recall, was:

"Ppphhhh! Bugger the driverless hozirontal evelator, that's what I say!!"

"Hurrah", we said, an one.

And that's about the last I remember. I vaguely recall a queue at the payphone, where every conversation seemed to include the same words:

"No, dear, absolutely impossible to get out. Car's in a snowdrift, old gel. What? Ah yes, a few other fellows here queuing for the phone – that's probably the noise you can hear, darling. Clinking of glasses? Ooh, noo, noo, I'm in the department, sweetheart – must be the snow on the window, dear. Hic. Hm, seem to have lost her."

The odd thing was, none of us students had a car. In fact, we all lived on campus. In fact, I'm pretty sure I could see my room from the bar. Well, I had to spend my generous grant on something, and when you're 50 miles from anywhere, you don't have a lot of choice.

Now, I wouldn't want to give you the impression that the cream of Britain's postgraduate engineers comprised a bunch of drunks. However, I cannot escape the fact that we were on several occasions actually paid to drink. To excess actually, and on three occasions to be precise. Well, quite a lot of research goes into driving behaviour and quite a lot of that goes into drunk driving. Quite right too: it's a dangerous menace and no two ways about it. So, to generate the observations for this research, somebody somewhere has to volunteer to get drunk and drive. The notice went up one afternoon on the Centre for Transport Studies noticeboard (can't think why), and the list of volunteers was finally complete after, I would say, about 45 seconds.

It worked like this. Every Tuesday lunchtime (in my case) for three weeks, you were left alone in a small room with a pint glass of orange-coloured liquid for some 30 minutes, during which time you had to drink the liquid. At the end of the 30 minutes, a nervous man in a crash helmet opened the door and led you to the airfield (the college was on an old war-time aerodrome), where he directed you into the driving seat of an old Austin Maxi, while he himself edged into the passenger seat. Having issued you with your own crash helmet, and checked the solidity of the vehicle's roll-bars, this brave man then asked you to drive out into the middle of the runway, this being a convenient hundred yards or so from the nearest immovable structure, and then to undertake a series of interesting tests, such as driving at exactly 20, then exactly 40, then exactly 60 mph past carefully positioned, but rather mangled, red-and-white cones. You performed these little tests with, variously: equanimity, a certain detachment or, frankly, recklessness. A key item of data collected was, of course, the contents of this week's orange-coloured liquid.

One time it consisted entirely of orange juice; another of 25% vodka; and the other of 50% vodka. The sequence was random for each test subject... although I have to say that after about ten minutes in that room, you began to get some inkling of which one it was.

For this little test, you got paid £6 per session. Plus, of course, for two Tuesdays in the term you had to borrow someone else's notes for the afternoon lectures. I don't know how much the passenger got paid, except that it wasn't enough. For my third stint, which incidentally was after an unscheduled two-week delay while they rebuilt the Maxi and repainted one side of the control tower, I noticed that it was a different chap.

I swear I am not making a single word of this up. I even know one of the conclusions of the research, which was that, at least for a sample of postgraduate Transport students, drinking alcohol *improves* your driving ability. It was something to do with the perceived need to look elsewhere than the speedometer when driving down the middle of a runway. The researcher got her PhD anyway, more for the methodology of her research than the results, I believe.

Another diversion from the actual work during this course was the college's free sports facilities. These also tended to support the revolutionary educational theories outlined in the previous chapter[37]. Back at school in Long Eaton, you'll recall, I'd been forced to take part in numerous barbaric sports, including rugby and cross-country running, thus initiating a life-long distaste for them. At Cranfield, however, where sport was optional and, as it happened, where my bony little body told me it was finally ready for a little rough and tumble, I spent hours and hours having a go at virtually everything – tennis, squash, cricket, table football, fancy-dress baseball – and kept most of them up for years afterwards... because we *chose* to do them, you see. The game that gripped the department, however, was six-a-

---

[37] Note here how easy it is, when a full-time student, to employ this pompous academic style in all one's writing, including in silly, self-indulgent memoirs. For proof, see footnotes.

105

side football. I don't know why, since we were quite hopeless at it. Maybe that's why.

Rescued from a noticeboard at the time, the report below on the valiant efforts of Centre for Transport Studies 'B' (the A-team weren't much cop either) will hint at the passion these events engendered:

CTS 'B' Undefeated Shock
CTS 'B' 0, School of Management 0

CRANFIELD, Friday

A capacity crowd of 12 saw CTS 'B' extend their unbeaten run in the college six-a-side tournament to one game here today by holding a well-dressed, well-groomed but well overrated Management side to a goalless draw.

In the early minutes, as Management piled on the – for want of a better word – pressure, they were foiled again and again by CTS's – for want of a better word – plan of forcing them wide, letting them panic and picking the ball out of the ditch. But the pattern changed when the Management defence was sent reeling (that dance band should never have been allowed on the pitch), by a move so simple it could only have been played by CTS. Gibson, Cannell and Garland combined with Deceptive Ease (a late substitute) to threaten the Management 'keeper, but fortunately the referee couldn't hear and play carried on.

The highlight of the second half was the good-natured banter between the wisely partisan crowd and the – for want of a better word – referee, concerning his eyesight, parenthood, departmental leanings and other items of topical interest. Management managed to graze the CTS crossbar with one shot that found CTS 'keeper Guise temporarily in a different time-space dimension, and shortly after this came the best chance of the match. Management's central striker for once escaped the almost intimate attentions of Kemp and Cannell to break clear, and had time to pick his spot (squeeze his boil, scratch his nose etc.) before proving that Guise had indeed been using a protractor, by hitting the post. At the other end, Cannell almost got on the end of a Gibson ball that had back of the net and "Property of HM Remand Centre Cranfield" written all over it.

With two seconds to go, CTS player-manager Gibson made a shrewd decision by bringing on Cosmos Charles for Dave 'Don't give it to me – I'm shattered' Coates. With CTS just beginning to find their feet (a fairly crucial requirement), the referee's whistle was as mistimed as most of the Management tackles he failed to penalize.

After the match, a spy in the Management bath reported recriminations and Radox flying in all directions. Gibson commented: "We went out there to play football and I think that's what confused them."

Reuter S Cramp

Other equally biased reports were penned by E I Addio (Our Man on the Terraces) and Hugh L Neverwalkalone.

The Long-Running Affair, Episode 3

The originals not only of the Cranfield football reports but also of our dissertations were generated by typewriters. Remember those? Yes, this was still deep in the pre-PC era, and so ribbons and Tippex bottles – and even fountain pens and blotters – still adorned the student's desk. A couple of years ago, when visiting Nottingham University campus, I found myself in a student room again for the first time in over 20 years, and the PC, printer and Internet connection, though no doubt perfectly standard, seemed peculiarly out of place to me.

Back in 1979, however, we did have another small – but for me, significant – encounter with another giant IBM. While most students of Transport study the variety that carry people, a select group of four of us at Cranfield favoured the variety that carry things. Yes, just like the mini-roundabouts, somebody has to study trucks. What the four of us chose to study in particular for our MSc project was 'the travelling salesman's problem'.

A travelling salesman has, let's say, twenty calls to make in a day. The problem is: in what sequence should he make them to minimize driving time? Well, of course you could just plot them on the map and figure it out by eye. But what if some of his customers are closed at lunchtime? What if he has to mix drops and collections? What if it's not one van, but twenty and you have to figure this out every day? What if... well, OK, cutting straight to the point here – it's a classic little job for that big mainframe in the computer room, isn't it? Except at Cranfield it was a computer *building*. We trotted across there, our precious little vehicle scheduling program scribbled on the back of some envelopes and held tight in our fists, and took it in turn to type the little bugger into the Big Blue, which duly spewed it out as a series of those punched cards that I'd heard about but until this moment had never actually seen. There were lots of them and they made a satisfying clatter when you shuffled them into neat packs before securing them with rubber bands. They were also of course destined for the museum of technology, and in pretty short order too, though we didn't know that at the time. The significance of this latest IBM encounter for me, though, was that, after ten years of fannying about in the old employment stakes, it accidentally launched me into the job market with the label 'computer expert' flapping around my neck. And, like pushing a bemused Paddington Bear onto a travelator over whose handrail he couldn't see, this so-called computer 'expertise' launched me into 20 years of what you might call 'proper' jobs.

One Wednesday during the Cranfield year I'd been sober enough to travel down to London (a direction that people who are down there call 'up') to have a chat with the very gruff-voiced man who'd offered me £7,000 out of the blue. His name was Frank and after further offering me coffee and lunch, Frank offered me a job in his office, which, since it paid about twice what I'd been earning for sending steel girders and nappies to Stockholm, I felt in no position to refuse.

Frank's company was a large multi-national whose name I can't tell you, but, as one of their products forms a basic requirement of life on Earth, I felt pretty confident they'd survive. Frank's job was Transport Resources Manager. 'Resources' meant people, and especially HGV-driving-type people. 'Manage' meant manage to get rid of as many as you can. My job was Transport Resources Officer. 'Officer' meant sit in an office and figure out which drivers we can get rid of, and why. These interesting corporate objectives came from on high; specifically from someone so far on high that he'd convinced the board of directors that his salary should be linked to the 'resources' we saved. The fewer people there were in the basement of the castle, the more the king would earn. We didn't do badly, Frank, me and the rest of the team; and so the king of the castle kept appearing in the national business pages as being remarkably well-paid. So was I. And, in case you were wondering, my conscience was and is quite clear.

There was a lot of hoo-ha around this time (the early 1980s) about big companies making people redundant without caring about what happened to them; but personally I can't see why companies *should* care. What's more, I don't see why companies should mess about with all this pension stuff, nor indeed all this employment stuff. Everything would be much simpler – and millions of working hours could be diverted into something more useful – if all workers were freelance, and if either side wanted to terminate the contract then that should be the end of it. Even by 1979 I'd already changed jobs often enough and, if you're flexible about what you do and where you do it, it's no big deal. "On your bike!", as Norman Tebbit said around this time, and he was right. Mind you, it's about the only thing he and his boss *were* right about.

The Long-Running Affair, Episode 4

More interesting than mere humans, however, was the ever-changing world of bits and bytes into which I'd fortuitously fallen. During my time with Frank, the Big Blue mainframes were being challenged by the arrival of 'mini-computers' (still pretty big and most often still blue) and then the first 'micro-computers' (a sort of vomit-grey). When the company put on a short residential course in rural Buckinghamshire called 'Getting to Grips with the Micro', Frank sent me along as the youngest face in the department. I'm still not sure why computers are thought of as things for young people, but anyway, this little sojourn in the sylvan slopes of the Chilterns proved to be yet another breakthrough. However, the most significant event of those three days – and one whose recollection still makes me stop and stare into nothingness as the cold chill seeps down my back – occurred before we woke up on the second morning.

It was 8th December 1980. My radio alarm came on in the middle of the seven o'clock news. "… He was shot on the steps of the Dakota Building, where he lived with his wife Yoko and son Sean. A hospital spokesman later declared Lennon dead on arrival." By the time I'd stumbled to the window to watch the melting overnight snow drip from the branches, my eyes were full and I found I had to grip the sill to stay upright. I know I'm only one of millions, but John Lennon was my friend. As the news passed around, the corridors of our conference centre saw face after face that went first blank, then red, then moist. Breakfast was almost silent. The morning's first session was cancelled. For the rest of the day, voices stayed muted and fingers tapped limply over keys which the previous day had seemed to herald a bright new future for us all. A future without Lennon – and without the still-longed-for possibility of a Beatles reunion – wasn't quite the same future it had been the day before.

We did learn something, though: we learned BASIC. One reason that learning how to program a computer was seen in 1980 as a neat introduction to how to *use* a computer was that there was hardly any software available, at least any that didn't involve batting a square white ball from side to side of the screen[38]. Another was that to learn BASIC sounded like something suitably basic, rather than what it actually was: something BASICALLY UNNECESSARY.

So, when I returned to my 9th-floor office in West London, I knew what a bit and a byte were and how to get a computer to ask you your name and if you didn't answer 'Guise', to say 'Bye-bye' and log you out[39]. And that's about it, really. Strange to say, though, with this meagre knowledge, and with a brand new Commodore PET on my desk, I was suddenly the bee's knees of the Transport Department. Not just my boss, but my boss's boss (dubbed Buggerlugs by Frank), would now stick his head into my little cell as he passed, with such comments as "How's the computer whizz kid, today?" and "This room big enough for you, Richard?" and "You couldn't find time do the wife's WI notices on that machine, could you?"

Hmm. Odd. After all, that grey, tinny little PET wasn't much more than a glorified typewriter-cum-calculator that also played Blondie if you put the wrong cassette in. (The IT industry had progressed from paper tape with holes, through stacks of cards with holes to magnetic tape without holes.) The reason the micro-computer was held in such absurdly high regard by departmental managers, of course, was nothing to do with the technology at all, but with a subject much closer to the heart of Buggerlugs and his colleagues: office politics. While mainframes and minis came from the Systems Department's budget and were locked away in their temperature-controlled 'machine rooms', little micros came from anyone's budget and sat on anyone's desk. Power to the people, you see.

As the Transport Department's resident 'whizz-kid', I soon started getting invited to all sorts of meetings that dealt with all sorts of

---

[38] The first, and happily the last, computer game I've ever played. For the next 20 years, I always threw that packet marked 'Games' into the bin.

[39] I'm pretty sure this fiendish ruse kept the world's industrial spies out of my files for years.

subjects that were complete Greek to me, given my dullness in Scruff's and Fish's science classes: things like electric circuits and solenoid valves. Of course, the obvious reaction from a whizz-kid would have been to swot up on all this technical stuff and become a fully-fledged whizz person. In fact, I left.

Welcome to England

Anyway, three years is more than enough for anyone to commute from Slough to Brentford. Indeed, it's more than enough for anyone even to *live* in Slough – and even Slough was better than Windsor, where the town council kept spending my rates on gifts for some old queen up in the castle.

Let's face it: you either love the south-east of England or you're sane. I like to think I'm fairly sane (though still open to debate) and so the sunny East Midlands called me. In fact, a chap named Charles called me from sunny Loughborough, offering me more income, less cost and a company Ford Capri in return for taking the fear out of computers for transport managers (plus selling them some of his software while their guard was down). Would I like to swap a one-bedroom flat in Slough for a two-bedroom detached bungalow in the country? 90 minutes of hell on the M4 every morning for a cyclable jaunt down leafy lanes? No contest. I still don't understand why anyone lives down there at all, especially now it's twice as noisy and ten times more expensive than then.

Charles' software house was chock-full of characters and one of them was an amiable Frenchman called Thierry. Thierry had been installing swimming pools for rich young women in Provence when he suddenly realized what he was missing and rushed north to work in a dank little computer room in a Burton-on-Trent brewery. (Don't ask.) A few days after his arrival, he'd walked down to Burton police station and presented himself at the desk with the very same words (and accent) that Clouseau himself would have chosen:

"Good morning. I 'ave arrived from ze city of Nice and I wish to register myself, sir, if you please."

Now, to any native French person, this would seem a perfectly reasonable request, but the desk sergeant simply stared for a while. Thierry repeated:

"I 'ave arrived. I must register myself."

The sergeant decided to try some lateral thinking.

"Do you want to register your dog, sir?"

"I 'ave no dog, sir, but that which I 'ave is a zhob."

"Which is?"

"I repair ze faulty computers in ze breweree."

"Ah good."

After another uncomfortable silence, Thierry resumed:

"I 'ave ze zhob. I need ze permit. For ze permit, I need ze register."

"Ah, I see, sir. Well, you don't need a permit to work here – you're French, aren't you, sir?" (Probably an unnecessary question.)

"I arrive from ze city of Nice in France."

"Well, the French don't need a work permit."

Thierry shifted his weight and examined the floor. This was a strange state of affairs indeed, since everyone in his own country, regardless of nationality, needed permits for every conceivable activity from birth to death, including birth and death. The sergeant glanced at his watch.

"Um", he ventured, "I hereby give you permission to work at the brewery."

Thierry's face lit up and he grasped the sergeant's hand, shaking it vigorously.

"Merci… thank you, sir. Thank you! But still I am not registered in England. You need my address."

Getting the idea now, the sergeant drew himself into a suitably imposing stance and said: "Your name, sir?"

"Thierry Boulot."

"Your address?"

"23 Rochford Street"

"I believe you, Monsieur Boulot. Welcome to England!"

With that, he found his hand again shaken enthusiastically by Thierry, who then turned to walk back onto Burton High Street with the sprightly step of a legitimate alien.

Thierry told me this tale when, a few years later, I was about to emigrate to France – in order to alert me to the administrative rigours that would lie ahead. If anything, things had got worse since Thierry was installing his pools.

Still back in England and in the early 1980s, though, I was proving to be probably the world's worst salesman. Too honest by far. Odd then, that this period was to see my only experience on the wrong side of the law, when I was arrested for interfering with a road sign.

The Law of Sartorial Rationality

National politicians are perverse little buggers. You[40] elect them into office to ensure the hospitals have enough bandages, the schools teach children about apostrophes and the police pick up the drunks before they[41] vomit through your letter-box. Instead they invade the Falkland Islands. At least the Argentinian government had the decency to collapse afterwards; the equally out-of-order British government went from mysterious strength to mysterious strength.

And that's not all. When another government keeps pointing nuclear missiles at your country, what would *your* reaction be? Well, going over to ask them why on earth they're doing it would be a good start. Campaigning in the United Nations for a ban on anyone pointing any nuclear missiles at anyone else would be a good follow-up. Thatcher? She takes money away from the hospitals, schools and police to build more nuclear missiles and point them back. Perverse *and* dangerous. So perverse and dangerous in fact that hundreds of thousands of people got rather cross and started sewing gaily coloured banners out of bedsheets. Oddly enough, Thatcher didn't crack under this sewing threat.

In the various CND groups I joined, I suggested a better strategy than sewing might be to meet some of the millions of otherwise normal people who thought that paying taxes to threaten innocent people just like themselves was a good investment, and try to talk sense into them. I tried it myself – at local clubs, in pubs, on doorsteps – and, though I usually met with the same "We didn't beat the Germans only to be invaded by the Russians" kind of drivel, at least I was making what seemed a relevant response. 90% of the CND members, though, persevered with their preferred strategy of sewing

---

[40] You, as in not me. I'm proud to say that no-one I've voted for has ever got in. Anywhere.

[41] The drunks, not the police.

the banners, plaiting their hair, wearing multi-coloured hats and juggling in the street. I couldn't see it myself.

In fact the 1980s convinced me of a Law of Sartorial Rationality, which, so far as I can see, has continued to operate to this day:

In politics, the sense of your policies
is inversely proportional to the sense of your dress.

However, just to show willing, I did take part in those marches and blockades at the various weapons sites. Despite the jugglers, we were fairly well organized and had plenty of legal advice before the events. At RAF Newton, Notts, which was rumoured to be a logistical support base for US missile operations (a rumour probably started by CND – I accept this), we were issued with big sticky labels that bore the initials 'USAF' to place over the road signs that said '*RAF* Newton'. In doing so, I was the one the police picked on to caution and a few weeks later received my summons to Bingham Magistrates' Court.

The potential fine was no problem, since CND collections covered these. What mattered was how I conducted myself in court, and so I had all my arguments and statements at the ready; but, strange to tell, I didn't need any of them and felt I won the battle on a technical knock-out. Constable Savage read out his charge of 'obscuring a road-sign on the public highway'. Bemused, I countered that changing 'RAF Newton' to 'USAF Newton' altered only two characters, leaving eight unchanged and still visible – an action that didn't in my view constitute 'obscuring'. The magistrate agreed and called Savage and me to the bench.

"Is this the correct charge, constable?"

"Er, I'm not sure, sir."

"Then I'll tell you, constable: it is *not*. A more reasonable charge would have been '*interfering with* a road sign', a charge on which, Mr Guise, I feel obliged to point out I would most probably find you guilty."

"Yes, sir," I ventured, "so would I."

"Now, to change the charge would involve abandoning today's proceedings, bringing new proceedings and incurring another five weeks' delay, not to mention the additional expense. You may force us to do that, if you wish, Mr Guise, but you may also choose a 'guilty' plea today and save us all the trouble."

114

Feeling rather pleased at having the outcome placed in my own hands, and of course having the cash for the £50 fine already folded neatly in my pocket, I breathed slowly, looked for several seconds into Constable Savage's reddening face and said: "I think the law has enough real crime to deal with to be bothered with honest citizens like me. Guilty as charged, sir."

Fortune favours the righteous.

VT Day

With hindsight, I wish I'd devoted at least some of my long hours of anti-Thatcher activities to another of the woman's insane policies, and one whose grim effects, as it turned out, would be even more widespread than those of either The Falklands War or nuclear proliferation. I'm talking about the privatization of the railways.

The Conservative member for Staines
Was short in the department of brains.
At Caius he read comics,
Not micro-economics,
And then he privatized trains.[42]

It's not very complicated. If resources are to be rationally allocated in the world, the price someone pays for something should be as close as possible to the marginal cost of producing it, where 'cost' means not just the money cost to the producer but also the effective cost to other people and to the environment. Once you've built a railway network, and are operating the trains on it, the marginal cost of taking an extra passenger is very low, much lower for example than the marginal cost of that same passenger undertaking the same trip by car, where the marginal costs include the fuel used, the wear and tear on the car and the environmental costs of having an extra car on the road.

The bottom line is that train fares need to be kept relatively low. However, a privately run railway needs to cover not just marginal costs but total costs, these latter including the cost of maintaining the network, providing the stations, funding research and development, and so on. So a *privately* run railway would tend to charge fares that make economic sense to itself, but are too high to make economic sense to the world in general.

So, just on economic grounds, the railways form a classic case of an industry justifying government intervention. Add to this the inherent need for central management in a physical network and you have a clear-cut case for nationalization – in less than a page!

This is not rocket science, not even Stephenson's Rocket science, but even this seemed beyond the grasp of the 1980s Conservative Party, blinded as it was by the apparently hypnotic aura of That Woman. So Britain's railways were privatized; so it soon cost more to travel by train from the East Midlands to London than to fly from the East Midlands to Spain; so Britain's roads soon became even more congested; so terrible rail accidents followed one after the other; so people avoided the railways like the plague, preferring a ten-mile

---

[42] From the author's 'Limerick Gazetteer of Great Britain'. Yes, I know the Minister of Transport wasn't the member for Staines nor studied at Caius: poetic licence.

116

traffic jam to possible death on the tracks; so the rail network faced financial collapse and Britain, where railways had been invented, suddenly possessed the most expensive, the most inefficient and the most dangerous system in Europe. And some numbskulls still think the sun shines out of Thatcher's voluminous backside.

When on 13th November 1990 the miracle happened, when Geoffrey Howe's speech prompted that unforgettable headline "Sheep bites back", and when That Woman finally resigned, I was working in Grenoble. Word passed round the office among the Brits like wildfire and the French seemed a little bemused to see a dozen of us at the *coin café* jumping up and down like, well, Continentals and waving sheets of paper with 'VT' (Victory over Thatcher) scrawled on them. That evening we bought copies of every English newspaper we could get our hands on and took them down to the Tonneau bar, where wine was ordered, scissors produced and every photograph of Thatcher we could find cut out. We then placed them face up along the tram track that ran in front of the bar. As the wheels of the big blue tram sliced through those evil features, fluttering page after page of a gloriously deformed ex-prime minister over the Place Notre Dame, we cheered and cheered and cheered until we were hoarse.

And she's still drawing a pension. Just wait for the celebrations when she dies.

The Long-Running Affair, Episode 5

While government policy was getting more and more insane, computers were getting more and more sensible. A PC had come to mean something other than a man in a tall black hat or a picture of the Golden Gate Bridge.

Back in 1982, I'd been one of the self-confessed nerds that arose before dawn to watch a man with a beard and a flowery shirt tell me what to do with my BBC Micro, Model A. This included drawing coloured lines on the TV screen... and nothing much else actually. By 1985, I'd graduated to an Apricot. A what? Exactly, but in those fruit-filled days of personal computing, Apricots seemed like Britain's answer to Apples and my little Apricot F2 boasted a remarkable little feature that still seems stunning today: there were no cables.

Yep, that's right. It had a full-size, infra-red keyboard and even an infra-red mouse, both of which worked fine so long as you didn't put

117

your coffee mug in the way of those spooky old rays. A more serious handicap, however, was the hard disk – in that there wasn't one. Yes, not only all the data and all the software but also the operating system itself sat on one of the floppies you could load into the two little slots. One afternoon, when I politely asked my Apricot if I could save the WordStar[43] file I was writing, the little fruit-face declined – no disk space, mate. So I deleted a few things, then a few more, then... well, OK, I'll cut straight to the quirky bit. Before I could save what I'd been writing, I had to delete most of the operating system itself *and the screen driver!* If you've never tried to communicate with a computer just by listening to its clicks and whirrs, then I can recommend it – like yoga, it does wonders for your powers of concentration, but also leaves you with shaky hands and a bad back.

However, Charles' Loughborough software house, having a bit more money than I, bought some real PCs for me to carry around to those potential customers that didn't have them, i.e. all of them. I can report that lugging a 1980s PC, complete with monitor, up the eight flights of stone stairs in a Tyneside flour mill is excellent for your thighs, though the dense clouds of flour are less excellent for the PC – and for your temper when the little tinker won't boot up.

OK, you've been very patient. No more computer tales till you've had a break in the sun. How does the South of France sound? When, one damp January morning in 1989 on an overcrowded high-speed train, I spotted an advert for a job in Grenoble on the back of someone else's Daily Telegraph, it sounded, well, tempting. So I bought the 'paper at the next station, applied for the job the next day and, well, got it... otherwise I wouldn't be banging on about it.

---

[43] Remember that?!

13. Though surrounded by mountain ranges (top: Vercors, right: Chartreuse, bottom: Belledonne), Grenoble is the flattest city in France. Taken from a Barcelona-Stuttgart flight, 1994. *Photo: author*

7

Sutty's Tale

Sutty and the Brain Drain

It was July 1989. Thatcher was still rampant, England's cricketers were not, and – since neither situation showed any sign of righting itself – I left.

It's not entirely true that cricket and politics were the sole forces driving me onto the 6 a.m. ferry to Calais. Money and boredom were involved too. And being too well known in a village too small. But anyway, I was away. I doubt I could claim to be part of the brain drain, only that I was marginally better at brainwork than drainwork. However, I was leaving a grey office job in the grey East Midlands for what would surely be an exotic office job in the exotic South of France. For ever, for all I knew.

I didn't leave alone. I crossed the Channel that misty summer morning with my faithful Toyota Corolla, and this chapter is his story.

I bought Sutty in 1988. His predecessor was his brother Charlie, also a Corolla, and Charlie's predecessor was a bicycle. I drive Toyotas because I don't like cars. Cars are the third most disagreeable subject that anyone could raise in a public bar (after children and mortgages). If anyone in my local tried to strike up a conversation with me by mentioning the internal combustion engine and calling it a "motor", I would suddenly find an excruciating need to visit the Gents, and then emerge in the lounge bar, getting the friendly barman to pass over my pint from the other side.

Cars are noisy, smelly and unreliable machines, and so am I. There's room for only one scumbag in a relationship and so my car has to be un-carlike. Toyotas are quiet, clean and, above all, reliable. For someone like me, who is allergic to whatever all that gubbins is under the bonnet, they are ideal. You just don't need to get involved.

So anyway, Sutty and I were made for each other, and we made a deal: he would refrain from breaking down, and I would take him to interesting parts of the world. Which brings us back to the plot. The RAC in Nottingham had told me that the only concession needed for the Land of Garlic and Charles Aznavour was to make Sutty's headlights yellow and stick a bit of black plastic on them.

As it turned out, from a technical point of view they were quite right. Having driven through France in the daylight, I did the little sticky-back plastic bit in a carport overlooking the rolling hills of Grasse, surrounded by lavender fields and fig trees, and with the help of some rather good Muscat. (You'll notice that, within 48 hours of arriving on the Continent, I'd turned from working-class slob into middle-class snob. I make no apologies for this, since we're talking Provence before Mayle here and, in any case, I only read his book a lot later, when desperate for reading material on the Sunset Limited, near Reno, Nevada. You see, there I go again.)

Sutty looked cool in his yellow and black shades. They were destined to last over five years, but I don't think they were designed to. As well as looking cool, Sutty still looked English, which is why, I suppose, he managed to get himself broken into on the riverbank in Grenoble. By this time I was a local resident, but Sutty wasn't, and the British plates were as good as a flashing neon arrow to *le voleur infernal* (literally, "the thieving bastard"). He got my radio, my camera, my briefcase and – worst of all – my filofax. Look, I've told you, this was 1989 – all right?

So, apart from the wrangle with the English insurance company about why I was writing to them from a French address when I was on a temporary green card, I spent much of the next few months phoning friends to ask them the phone numbers of other friends. When this is the first time for several months you've spoken to someone you used to play squash with twice a week, it's a hell of a job making them realise the size of French phone bills.

"Bonjour, it's Richard here, calling from France."

"Reeecharr! Hey, how's it goi ... I mean, comment allez-vous?"

"Oh well, not bad, but someone broke into the car and stole ..."

"Oh no! I mean, sacré bleu! What a bummer! I say, what's the French for bummer?"

"Well, I haven't got that far actually. Look, the thing is, they stole my filofax and ..."

"Aha! Steph, did you hear that, old Guisey's had his filofax nicked in France. Hey, Reeecharrr, didn't we tell you ...."

Etc etc.

But apart from this slight misdemeanour, Sutty behaved pretty well for a Japanese-Englishman abroad. He kept to the right side of the road; he didn't complain when Renault 5s stopped dead in front of him while their owners dashed into a Depot of Pain; he didn't confuse the traffic by stopping at pedestrian crossings; in other words he pretty much went native. So, as a reward, I decided to make him legal. In fact, on reflection, it might have been easier if I'd told the authorities that I wanted to register my Japanese wife.

I just wanted to register my car.

Sutty Conquers France

"Vos papiers, s'il vous plaît, monsieur".

This is the call of that not so rare species, the French petty official. They are everywhere and they're all called Monsieur Poncet, except when they're called Madame Poncet or Officer Poncet. They are from the same stock as the wartime Gestapo on the look-out for escaped prisoners of war, and they have the same inferiority complex. The call really means: "I know you are a wiser and more important human being than me, but in order for you to reside in my country / work in my town / have my dustmen collect your rubbish etc, you need this piece of paper from me; and before I sell it to you, you are going to be severely ... er ... inconvenienced ... damn, I wish it was still the thumbscrews ... ah, the old days ... etc etc."

Registering your car in France is a tough enough assignment for the French themselves when they move house from one *département* to another, but with a foreigner, and with a foreign car to boot ... well, this is like manna from heaven for the Poncets. However, it can be done. Indeed, theoretically it *must* be done within six months of your vehicle's arrival in France. Sutty's encounter with *le voleur infernal* prompted me to start well before the deadline.

Waiting for Poncet

First things first. What I was after was a *carte grise*, so called because it's a card and it's grey. This is the French vehicle registration document. The French authorities refer to a foreign registration document as a *carte grise étrangère*, on the touching assumption that all overseas documents must be mere copies of their own. If, when Officer Poncet pulls you over to the side of the road and bleats his call, you offer him a blue and white British registration document, he will look at it as a monkey looks at a mysterious monolith from another world.

Anyway, I'd heard a rumour that foreigners registering cars should present themselves to the *Service des Douanes* (customs office), in the centre of town. I did so one bright October afternoon. Madame Poncet was behind a glass window. She told me to wait on the little chair in the draught by the door, until Monsieur Poncet was free. I could see Monsieur Poncet sitting in a warm office at a big desk in front of a big map of the world, access to which he controlled. He was alone, so I knocked and entered. He told me to wait on the draughty chair until he was free. When I was suitably frozen, he beckoned me in. I told him I just wanted to register my car and noticed a sinister twinkle in his eye at the word "just". He gave me a kind of checklist of what I had to do, which I thought was jolly decent of him, and pointed to the *Service des Mines* at the top of the list.

The *Service des Mines* is an office conveniently located in a camouflaged portakabin hidden up a dirt track in the middle of an area of desolation about three miles out of town. I wondered where the mines came into it. In French 'mine' means either a mine, a pencil lead, or a facial expression. It was clear on arrival at the *Service des Mines* that this was the local office of the Ministry of Expressions. Madame Poncet glowered at me from behind her bullet-proof glass. I said I just wanted to register my car and she stiffened at my foreign accent, saying that aliens should go to the *Service des Douanes*. When I showed her Monsieur Poncet's list with the Ministry of Expressions at the top, she ruefully admitted that she was indeed involved, but that the list was not necessarily in chronological order, rather simply a checklist of things to be done. I had clearly fallen for Monsieur Poncet's little trick. She told me that I first needed a *timbre fiscal*, which was presumably a medieval percussion instrument. I asked her to sell me one, but she said that I had to go to a tobacconists. This whole episode was assuming the air of one of those dreams you have after a cheap curry.

Feeling that it had been a while since I'd spotted a medieval instrument section in a tobacconists, I took the precaution of asking a colleague at work about this *timbre fiscal*. It turns out to be a stamp used for tax purposes. Ah yes, I remembered something about fiscal policy in Economics classes at Derby Technical college – things were beginning to fall into place at last. But the tobacconists? It also turns out that the French *tabac* is part of a government scheme to cut down the queues in post offices by turning tobacconists into pretend post offices. Of course, this just moves the queues to the *tabacs*.

I waited for 15 minutes in a pretend post office queue at my local *tabac*, to get my 120-franc *timbre fiscal*. Madame Poncet was serving. She said "120 francs?! You'll have to go to the post office for that, dearie." (Or at least I took it from her tone that "dearie" is the English equivalent of whatever she called me.) I went to the real post office. They told me to go to the *Préfecture*.

The Grenoble *Préfecture* in Place de Verdun is an enormous building with enormous queues that make those at the *tabac* look like a child's game. As well as the queues, there is always an assorted rabble of miscreants milling about or lounging on benches. All in all, it looks like a pickpockets' convention. Keeping my hand on my wallet, I scanned around and, lo and behold, there was a desk marked "timbres fiscaux", with no queue. Ignoring the trap of the perverse plural, I sauntered up, asked for a 120 franc t.f., got one and exited smartly.

It was by then two weeks since I had met Monsieur Poncet of the *douanes*, I had visited five offices in and around Grenoble, and it was snowing; but I had earned the right to tick off one item on my checklist, which I did with a flourish, and I was beginning to warm to the challenge. The Poncets might just have met their match.

I returned to the Ministry of Expressions and thrust my *timbre fiscal* towards Madame Poncet's superior face. She gave me a wad of documents, one of which was called *Demande de Certificat d'Immatriculation*. I took them home and studied them. The DCI asked for the sort of technical details about my car that would probably require a visit to the factory in Yokohama, where I would find that they were locked in a steel vault under the 24-hour

125

protection of a guard from the Japanese Anti-Espionage Squad. It was a nightmare. I took the DCI to my French teacher. She said it was a *cauchemar*. At least my French was improving.

I went back to the Ministry of Expressions and threw myself on Madame Poncet's mercy. She gave me a withering look and called over a man in a boiler suit and crash helmet, clearly a Grand Prix driver who'd fallen on hard times. Didier Pironi came out with me to take a look at Sutty. He scribbled a few oily marks on my DCI and gave it me back. I took it home and studied it. Apparently Sutty has a surface area of 16.7 square metres, and is a *Berline*. Surely Monsieur Pironi didn't mistake Sutty for a Mercedes!

My next task was to return to the *Service des Douanes*. I did my time on the draughty seat until I got the call from Monsieur Poncet and his world map and presented him with my impressive bundle of papers about the car. He said these were the wrong papers He didn't care about the surface area of my Corolla.

He wanted me to try and prove that.

- I was who I claimed to be.

- I was a genuine French resident.

- I owned the car that I claimed to have brought into his country.

Now I understood Thierry's bewilderment at the Burton-on-Trent policeman's touching credulousness. Assuming that Monsieur Poncet's constant references to 'claiming' things were his little way of throwing down the gauntlet, I accepted the challenge and went home to seek out these other papers, which, according to Monsieur Poncet, I should in any case carry on my person at all times. It was a fruitless search. All I could come up with was my passport and my *carte de séjour* (residence permit).

I went back and offered these to Monsieur Poncet the map. He was disdainful. My *carte de séjour*, itself gained only after an hour's interrogation at the police station, was not good enough because, you see, what a *customs* official wants are *customs* papers. Some pathetic little form issued by the *gendarmes* is not good enough. Monsieur Poncet wanted to see the documents I had had stamped when I entered France.

"Documents? Stamps? I just drove through – nobody stopped me."

"What?! How long ago?"

"Six months ago."

"What?!!"

I thought Monsieur Poncet was going to have a seizure. Some foreigner had just driven into his country with all his worldly goods, rented a flat and got a job, all without any French customs papers! "Why should I register your car, monsieur? You might just be here on holiday!"

I thought, "What kind of pervert do you think I am, spending a six-month holiday traipsing around all the public offices of Grenoble? Do you think I come here for the pleasure of your company, you old fool?"

I said: "Would it help if I declared everything now, monsieur?"

His eyebrows responded to my olive branch, for, after staring at me for several seconds, and with a sigh but no words, he pulled a sheaf of papers from his left-hand drawer. For a good ten minutes, he filled boxes on them in a careful script, occasionally asking me in a monotone about my date of arrival, the value of my chattels, and so on. He then took from his right-hand drawer a rubber stamp, and, fixing me now with a steely gaze, let loose his wrath in a flurry of paper stamping. Every page received at least four vicious stampings, and I noticed that his desk top received two errant blows in the blur of rubber weaponry.

He handed me the pulverised paperwork and confirmed that he was "à votre service". Muttering my thanks, I left, hoping that I wouldn't need to visit this Monsieur Poncet again.

Amongst the heavily stamped documents was a green customs certificate. This was the entry requirement for my next call – to the *Contrôle de Sécurité*.

This is the garage where you get your foreign car tested as being fit for French roads (unlike most French cars). Being a mechanic's environment, the *Centre* has no Messieurs Poncets and so, after just a cursory examination of Sutty and his paperwork, they added another certificate to my pile and bid me "bon courage".

Then it was back to the Ministry of Expressions again to ask a particularly lugubrious Madame Poncet if she'd be so kind as to open a dossier for me, now that – after two months' hard graft – I could show enough papers to demonstrate that I was serious. I was now getting wise to the system and had perused my dog-eared checklist before departure, so that included in the bouquet of papers that I offered to Madame P were Sutty's purchase invoice and an electricity bill (don't ask why). She thumbed through the stack and twitched her right eyebrow in a positive direction as she opened a dossier with Sutty's name and mine on the cover and booked us in for a session with Didier Pironi the following Wednesday afternoon.

As I later settled down to a beer to celebrate the upturn in my fortunes, I suddenly saw the trap I'd fallen into. I'd made my latest visit to the Ministry of Expressions by bicycle, since Sutty was now uninsurable. My British insurance company wouldn't look at me since I'd lived abroad too long for their liking; my French insurance company wouldn't look at me because I hadn't got a French registration. But in order to get a French registration, I had to drive on the French highway to get Sutty to the Ministry of Expressions. Voilà - catch *vingt-deux*! I now realised that the mysterious knots of people seen deep in conversation in any French café late at night are in fact gaggles of Poncets plotting the downfall of any innocent alien threatening to breach their red tape. Aha! Well this time they'd chosen the wrong alien to mess with – I'm British, damn it, and it'd take more than a bunch of Mediterranean morons to corner me!

Little did they know it, but I'd kept a photocopy of each and every document on my route so far. I now gathered these together and started a tour of the Grenoble insurance offices. It didn't take long to find a flexible friend whom I could convince that, with this paperwork, I would one day conquer not only the Poncets of Grenoble but possibly the world, and do so without even thinking about rear-ending a BMW. Armed with my little French insurance sticker, I reported to Monsieur Pironi.

Something was distracting Didier as he checked Sutty's chassis number. When he fumbled with the ignition key at the start of the test drive I knew what it was – the rare prospect of a spin in a right-hand drive car. Sutty didn't know what had hit him. Didier tore round the dirt track surrounding the Ministry's portakabin like a man possessed and on the third circuit I caught a glimpse of his eyes through the dust: they were the eyes of a man reliving the 1976 duel with Fittipaldi at Silverstone. I was glad that the system insisted on the *Contrôle de Sécurité* before the car was aged ten years in two minutes.

Didier gave Sutty the thumbs up and we were asked to come back the following Friday for the dossier.

A final emotional visit to the Ministry of Expressions – had six months really passed since that first autumn afternoon when I chanced upon Madame Poncet's grim features? She handed over my completed dossier with a vicious leer and instructions to present myself once again at the *Préfecture*.

Back at the Préfecture, I was this time condemned to be a part of the riff-raff. I took my numbered ticket and sat down, wishing that, like the other loiterers, I'd brought along a copy of The Pickpocket Gazette to while away the time. After amusing myself for a while by growing a beard, I saw my number come up on the screen, and went upstairs to the desk indicated, where I passed over the secret papers from the Ministry. Madame Poncet de la Préfecture gave half of them back to me in disdain. She asked me to confirm that I owned the car, i.e. that I owed no money on it. They haven't yet invented a document which proves this for foreigners, and so she was forced to accept my word – the disappointment showed. Just out of spite, she asked to see my *carte de séjour*. Ha, no problem. With no more ideas on how to detain me further, she gave me a little pink card and told me to wait until my name was called out downstairs at Desk A. Being now *rue*-wise enough not to waste time hanging around indefinitely in French government offices, I went for a beer and came back in an hour. I was by now easily beating the French at their own game, and scented victory. On returning to the *Préfecture* I ignored the clutch of spectators loitering around Desk A and marched up to a young Mademoiselle Poncet to ask if I'd had the call. Indeed I had, and so I presented to her my pink card. She lifted aloft my *carte grise* (for she had it!) and gave it to .... Desk B. Aaargh, so near! Scuttling round to Desk B, I gave Mademoiselle Poncet B my cheque for 630 francs and she gave me my carte grise.

Exit to Place de Verdun, punching the air.

How to Frustrate a French Flasher

So Sutty got his sexy little black number. He suddenly fitted into the environment as easy as pastis and garlic and, lined up in the company car park, he looked quite at home with the 2CVs, 205s and the other *sacrés numéros*.

On the road, however, it was a different matter. You see, there was still the little matter of the steering wheel being on the wrong side, or rather on the right side in both senses; but to these perverse continental types it looked wrong enough even with British plates, but with French plates ... well, it looked so wrong that the families in the overtaking Citröens and Renaults all went through the same predictable routine:

1. Garlicmobile approaches Sutty from behind as normal. (That is, at an illegal speed and with headlights flashing ... this is what passes for normal in France.)

2. Garlicmobile overtakes Sutty and driver casts suspicious glance at Sutty's empty driver's seat.

3. Garlicmobile driver makes smart remark over right shoulder to children in the back.

5. Garlicmobile slows down and pulls in front of Sutty.

6. Two snotty children's faces appear at Garlicmobile's rear window, grinning and sticking tongues out until Sutty's driver makes rude sign.

7. Garlicmobile pulls hastily away.

What I enjoyed even more was holding up the locals at the toll booths. France being relatively organised on the transport front, their car drivers have to pay for using the roads – a simple concept that Britain's simple politicians seem unable to grasp in the twentieth century. So there are plenty of toll booths. Toll booths on the left-hand side of the cars; toll booths where right-hand-drive cars without passengers have to stop while the driver unhooks his seat-belt, gets out, walks round, pays the dosh, walks back, waves at the queue behind, gets in, re-hooks his belt and eventually drives off; toll booths with perplexed Poncets puzzling both inside and outside the booths.

This was good enough fun even when the British plate should have warned them, but when my French plate gave me a perfect disguise ... well, it was a stunt almost worth paying the toll for. My favourite trick was to loiter around a mile or so before the toll, slowly overtaking some Trabant or other, and waiting for the inevitable moronic flasher to come zooming up in his Audi to within about a centimetre of Sutty's back bumper. I'd then pull in and let the *imbécile* overtake, but immediately accelerate for all I was worth in an attempt to re-take the flasher before the toll. If I made it, and got Sutty in front of him in the toll queue, I'd exaggerate every little action when my turn came to pay. I'd feign a problem getting unhooked, lazily saunter round to the booth, have a little chat with the tollstress, saunter back – maybe polishing the bonnet on the way – and, rather than just wave to the fuming flasher, stop and make an elaborate steering-wheel-type gesture while pointing at the car. I just love a French flasher when he's exhibiting *la rage de la route*.

But apart from such highlights – and also the one when the *gendarmes* pulled me and a passenger over because the driver appeared to be looking at the football pages instead of the road – Sutty cruised France for a couple of years without incident. Such success led me to believe that, when I decided to swap the *pastis* for *sangria* and head for Spain, switching Sutty's plates again would be a piece of *tortilla*. After all, this time he was already legalised in a left-hand drive country and, anyway, thousands of cars must move from France to Spain. Mustn't they?

So, one bright Sunday in Spring '92, I piled Sutty roof-high with my belongings, bade *adieu* to the Alps and set off confidently for the sun.

Part of my confidence came from the fact that, this time, I'd sussed out the customs procedures in advance. I'd collected a whole wad of certificates from the Spanish Consulates in London and Lyon – both in person, of course. (Yes, a British citizen living in the South of France and moving just across the border to the North of Spain still had to go in person to the Spanish Consulate in London to get permission ... and this was at a time when our glorious politicians were boasting about Europe's free movement of labour – another downright lie.) The Spanish gentleman at the consulate in Lyon, however, was most helpful, telling me in his stilted French: "At the point of entering the Spain, monsieur, you must demand of the officer of the customs the certificate of the importation of the goods."

Well, at the point of entering the Spain, atop the Pyrennean pass of le Perthus in fact, no-one paid any attention to the Corolla packed to the gunnels with what might well have been cocaine, but was in fact mostly books, non-fiction, etc. So I parked and walked over to the customs office, queued with the lorry-drivers taking frogs legs to Figueres, and then asked the *señor* behind the glass to stamp my list. His answer was definitely in the negative, but at the time I understood not a word of his language (indeed, I didn't even know he had two to choose from), and so I'd no idea why he couldn't do it, and just drove on, wondering when this shortfall in the old customs stamp department would come home to roost. It was destined to do so, in fact, some six months later, on the first floor of an ugly office block in downtown Barcelona, for it was that summer's Olympic city that was to be my new home.

Sutty Fails to Conquer Spain

Here is an intelligence test. Read the following sentence and then answer the questions below. This car is a Japanese make, purchased in England and brought into Spain by way of France.

Question 1: Where did I purchase this car?

Question 2: Where do you think the steering wheel is?

If you answered "Spain" and "On the left – where else could it be?", you should apply for a job with El RACC, who will welcome you with open arms. No wonder the Armada was a shambles. How the hell a few Spaniards managed to run most of South America for three centuries is one of history's unsolved mysteries. If those Inca people who used to build giant Legolands up in the Andes were as smart as they're supposed to have been, why did they get themselves conquered by a bunch of bulbous-trousered half-wits from Seville?

The Old Municipal Imposter

El RACC is the Royal Automobile Club of Catalunya, is pronounced 'El Rack', and was probably first established during the Spanish Inquisition. It's in downtown Barcelona and is a three-storey office at Santaló 8, with nowhere to park for miles around. This fact turned out to be important. I suppose it never occurred to El Rack's founding fathers that any of their members might actually want to drive there – "Drive to an automobile club? How absurd!" Quite. So when someone at my office gave me the tip-off as to El Rack's existence, I popped down on the train, taking off what turned out to be the first of many half-day holidays from work in pursuit of a Spanish vehicle registration for Sutty.

I entered the portals of Santaló 8 for the first time. In my poor[44] Spanish: "I wish to matriculate my English car in Spain. Where do I go?"

"Are you sociable?"

---

[44] A significant improvement on 'non-existent', you'll notice.

"Pardon?"

"Are you a sociable of El Rack?"

Seeing the light, "Ah, no, I'm not a member – I just want to know where is the correct office of administration."

"Ask across the street – No. 5."

"Gracias."

I crossed the street to No. 5, which also sported a RACC nameplate, and entered.

"I wish to matriculate my English car in Spain."

"Are you sociable?"

Here we go again. "No, I'm not a member of El Rack – I just want to know where is the correct office of administration."

"Ask across the street – No. 8."

"They have told me to come here."

A quick discussion with a colleague. " I have reason – ask at No. 8."

"Gracias."

Back at No. 8. "At No. 5, they have told me to return here."

A quick discussion with a colleague. "They have reason – go to the desk Servei de Gestoría."

Wondering why an Automobile Club might offer a Jester Service, I went where directed. "I wish to matriculate my English car in Spain." Rapidly I added: "I am not a sociable of El Rack. I just want to know where is the correct office of administration."

The young woman wrote down the address of *El Ministério del Interior – Jefatúra Provincial de Tráfico* and pushed it towards me, declaring in triumph "El Tráfico!"

"Er, do you know which papers are necessary?"

Her narrowing eyes indicated I was near the limit of favours for non-sociables, but she relented and passed me a photocopy of a photocopy of *Documentación Necesária*. Aha – the Spanish version of Monsieur Poncet's checklist! I was on my way.

El Tráfico is nowhere near a tube station and, as I hadn't yet figured out the routing of Barcelona's buses, I made my way back to work. At least I had something to go on and on the train I studied the vital list of *Documentación Necesária*. The usual stuff was there, though disguised in Spanish bureaucratese:

133

1. **The vehicle's documentation facilitated by the concessionary.** This sounded to me like the registration document or, translated into French bureaucratese, *le carte grise*! *Ça y'est!*

2. **DNI.** Ha ... trying to fool me with an unexplained acronym! But I happened to know that the poor old Spaniards have to carry around an ID all the time and this was it. Tough, I didn't have one – they'd have to make do with my James Bond passport.

3. **Impression of solicitude of matriculation.** I could do a very good impression of solicitude, but this sounded like an application form of some kind ... I do wish these foreigners would say what they mean.

4. **An 8000-peseta *tasa*.** Whatever a *tasa* was, and I suspected it wasn't a cup of tea, I was sure it would be of no use to me and had the feeling that it would turn out to be of much greater use to *El Tráfico*, who would duly relieve me of it.

5. **Autoliquidation of the old municipal imposter of circulation.** This one was going to be tricky.

The Dragon and the Rooster

Government offices in Spain are open only in the morning. Quite why is a mystery. I wonder if the prime minister, the king and the army all put their feet up by two o'clock as well? If any would-be invader is reading this, I strongly recommend mid-afternoon for the conquest of Spain – no resistance, no bloodshed, and I think you'll find the key to the parliament building on the hook in the concierge's office. Please clean up before you leave. Thank you.

El Tráfico is a government office and so I took another morning off work. It's on Barcelona's Gran Vía, which is not grand at all, just big and, on this occasion, awash with 500 white Seat Toledos, each carrying an Olympic official with a furrowed brow and a big watch. Also big is *El Tráfico*... and the queue outside when I arrived at 8:50 a.m., ten minutes before opening: it was several hundred yards long in fact and snaked around the block. No way: I cut my losses and drove back to work.

The next day I arrived at 1:50 p.m., ten minutes before closing. This was a better move. Fewer Toledos, no queue, but just a lot of world-weary punters trundling out of the building. I duly reported to the front desk with my usual plea "I wish to matriculate ...", did the usual bureau shuttle between various desks, all offering no information other than directions to another desk, until I landed at one where an old dragon offered me the old *Documentación Necesária* list.

"¡Aha!", I said, "Already I have it." My word order was becoming Hispanic and, by the way, I've just discovered the upside-down exclamation mark on this keyboard¡ "Furthermore, I have the things on the list!", I proclaimed, waving my impressive pile of papers and certificates for her appreciation. She was unappreciative.

"This car is an importation?"

"It's an English car, but I come to Spain from France."

"Have you the documentation of the customs?"

Yes, yes, this all sounded very familiar, but little did the old dragon know that I was an old hand at this kind of lark, having graduated from the Grenoble School of Bureaucrat Bashing. I triumphantly proffered my list of belongings brought from France, duly stamped by the Spanish Consulate in Lyon.

"This is just a list of belongings," she said.

I couldn't deny it. "But included is my car." I pointed out that, squeezed between "Books, non-fiction, 500" and "Records, Beatles, 100" was "Toyota Corolla, 1".

"This is no good." She was depressingly definitive. "Who will import your car?"

"I will."

My innocence was as evident as the dragon's world-weariness, as she gave me a heavy wad of customs documents. "You may return when is imported the car."

I slumped into a chair by the stairs and looked hopelessly through the awful customs forms. I'd been waiting for the border incident to come home to roost and, well, it had just flown in.

The Jesters of the Rack

At my next Spanish lesson, after debating with Esther, my teacher, whether Linford Christie had run the 100 metres final like 'una bala de una pistola' or 'una rata en un sumidero', I asked her what all these horrible questions on these horrible forms meant. She had no idea. Clearly I needed to use a jester, she said. A jester, Esther? These Catalans had clowns on the brain. She carefully explained the meaning and spelling of the word *gestor* and this turned out to be the most valuable addition to my Spanish vocabulary contributed by Esther, who, as it turned out, would be even more useful on the same subject a few months later.

A *gestor* is someone who works in a *gestoria*. So far so good. But what it actually is is harder to explain, for it's a job that doesn't exist anywhere else in the world but Spain, for the simple reason that it's not needed anywhere else but Spain. (Well, OK, maybe France could do with a 'gesteur', and what a powerful position it might be.)

A *gestor* is someone who knows every government office, every government official, every government form, all relevant opening hours and every queue's rush hour, for every government service in his or her town. This incredibly valuable information is for sale, in the form of a service, called *gestoria*. What these brave and tireless souls do is to represent you, the humble citizen, in your dealings with *el hermano grande*, be this big brother the fearsome government of Spain or the mysteriously vague, but even more fearsome 'Generality of Catalunya'. Or indeed the dragon at *El Tráfico*.

What a concept! And where, I asked Esther, might I find a suitable *gestor* to deal with the importation of the cars? Oh, she said, El RACC I should think! Aha! The Jester Service! So the woman behind the sign was one of them. No doubt I'd have to become a sociable of the rack, but so what?

This time I didn't need to take half a day off, as I was going on holiday anyway. I spent the first morning of these long-overdue hols down at Santaló 8 again, this time signing up with El Rack. Having paid my dues, got my window sticker and my Guide to Catalunya (all in Catalan – not much use to me, but the pictures are nice), and presented myself at the Jesters' Desk. It being the first time I'd ever knowingly seen members of this remarkable profession, I observed the jesters behind the desk with the same awe a boy of seven might reserve for gazing at an astronaut. Had I known what was ahead of me, I wouldn't have been so impressed.

"Good day. I am a sociable of El Rack", I announced, head held high, "and here is my card. I want to import my English car from France and matriculate it in Spain. Here is the history of the car. Can you do it?"

The young woman gave a cursory glance at the A4 sheet I had prepared the previous night – a masterpiece of colour graphics denoting quite brilliantly the history of both Sutty (Nottingham > Grenoble > Spanish border > Barcelona) and me (British resident > French resident > Spanish resident), complete with dates and a checklist of documents.

Alas, she dismissed my work out of hand and demanded the car's documents. Undeterred, I offered her photocopies of both Sutty's British and French registration documents. She rejected them both and demanded the original *carte grise*, which she must, she said, return to ... er ... "Grraynoblay". I handed it over, and everything else she asked for.

She on whom my hopes for Sutty's legality now rested spent the next 15 minutes poring over a set of papers at her desk. Much of this time was spent in a huddle with a fellow jester as they studied a thick reference book and eventually her expression grew worryingly graver as the minutes passed. Finally she came over.

"Señor, your car does not exist."

"Oh dear, and I've been driving it around for four years and it doesn't exist!" Sarcasm was clearly not in the repertoire of Catalan jesters and anyway I knew she meant that there was no such model in Spain. "I'm not surprised. It didn't exist in France either. In France, they identified a similar car and used that."

More huddled discussion. Eventually: "We have identified a similar car and used that."

"Congratulations."

"You must pay for the importation of the car 48,000 pesetas."

Resort to calculator. Two hundred and fifty quid?! That's outrageous! A thought which had been floating around my mind for some time popped to the surface. "What if I wait until January 1st 1993? The frontier between France and Spain will disappear, no?"

"Maybe, señor."

"Will the 48,000 disappear?"

"Many persons have asked this question, señor. No person knows the answer."

Nevertheless, it was worth the chance. "I shall wait."

I retrieved my papers and retreated. What had I to lose? In fact, what I had to lose was the use of my car for six weeks. In case you were wondering, the only reason I was trying to register my car was to be able to insure it. I didn't give a damn about the stupid Spanish registration, but, with the alarming driving behaviour in Barcelona, driving around uninsured would be foolhardy as well as illegal. I was in the same hole as in Grenoble, but this time neither Britain nor France would insure me because I was a Spanish resident, and Spain wouldn't insure me because Sutty wasn't. Catch *veíntidos*.

Resolving to resume the bureaucratic battle in a few months' time, I took myself off to the railway station for a fortnight improving my Spanish word order in Andalucía.

The Brassrubbers' Union

For the last six weeks of 1992, Sutty was off the road. Early in 1993, with frontiers tumbling all over Europe, I returned to El Rack. Straight to the Jesters' Desk. This time a young man approached.

"Good day. I am a sociable of El Rack ..." etc. Magnificent free A4 information sheet offered again and rejected again. "My car does not exist in your big book, but I suggest you identify a similar car and use that." Narrowing of jester's eyes, but otherwise compliance. I venture: "Er, it is 1993. There is no necessity to pay for the importation of the car, no?"

"There is no general importation tax, señor."

"Bravo."

"However, the Spanish government has imposed, from January 1st 1993, a special importation tax for cars which enter Spain."

"How much?"

"For your car, señor, 48,000 pesetas."

The bastards. If I had an MP, or even an MEP, a stinging letter, and maybe a death threat, would soon be winging its way to his office. However, this was post-single-market but pre-Maastricht-implementation, which – as I'm sure you fans of European legislation know (stop that yawn back there!) – meant I had no vote. I was one of the five million disenfranchised Europeans who were citizens of one country and residents of another. We had no vote in either until Maastricht became law. This partly explained my aggressive

138

reactions around this period to anyone who said a word against the Maastricht Treaty, i.e. all my friends. Belated apologies.

"OK, carry on."

I had given the jester all my English, French and Spanish documents I thought relevant. One in particular caused a dossier[45] of three jesters to gather around it. The young man eventually came over to me.

"Señor, we have your document in French which says that you have left France."

"Yes."

"We have your document in Spanish which says that you have arrived in Spain."

"Good."

"We need a document in Spanish which says that you left France."

I breathed deeply and counted to *diez*. "No such document exists", I managed in a calm monotone.

"But it is essential, señor. It is at your house?"

There have been many times during my sojourn in Spain when I longed for the mythical babel fish, which, when placed in anyone's ear, renders anything they hear into their own language. This was one of those times. If you know the Spanish for "you buffoon", please insert it where appropriate in my following, frustratingly weak, reply.

"I say again – it does not exist. French officials do not issue documents in Spanish. You have said that you know the French document says I have left France. Here we are in Spain, no? Do you see me? Here I am. Here is my resident's permit. I have left France.

"Mm, we shall try without this document, señor. However, we shall need a *frotamiento* of the number of the chassis of the car."

"*Frotamiento*?"

The jester took a blank piece of paper and a pencil and proceeded to move the pencil back and forth across the paper until he had shaded a neat arc. It dawned on me.

"You mean like on a tomb in a church?"

---

[45] I assume this to be appropriate collective noun.

139

Much laughter. "Exactly, señor." These people are indeed completely out of their tree. Just wait until the Poncets latch on to this ruse... they'll love it. Let's make all the foreigners do some brass-rubbing before we give them their *carte grise*. Ha bloody ha.

So I catch the train back home, open up Sutty's bonnet, find the chassis number (for it is there), do two brass-rubbings of it – much to the consternation of passers-by, catch the train back into Barcelona, march down to Santaló 8 and slam my artwork on the Jesters' Desk. It had taken four hours.

"Gracias. We shall call you, Señor Geesay."

They're all mad.

Bad News in Badalona

The call comes through after a few days. "Señor Geesay, we have your plates. Please to come to El Rack."

Another half-day holiday, but maybe this will be the last? Straight to the Jesters' Desk.

"You have my Spanish plates."

He hands them over. Spanish plates are white. The plates he gave me were green.

"These plates are green."

"Yes, señor, your eyes are good." Ooh, so they can be sarcastic when they try! "They are temporary plates."

"Temporary? Why?"

"Well, señor, you must of course first visit the *Industria*. We cannot issue permanent plates just like that."

I thought: "Just like that?! Listen, mate. I've been on the track of these damned fool plates for four months, have already used up half my annual holidays on these ridiculous jaunts to your conveniently located office, have given you all the official documentation I own – short of my badge from the 10th Long Eaton Cubs (1963 pack) – have committed myself to a king's ransom for nothing yet in return, and have even done a spot of gratuitous brass-rubbing. I don't call that 'just like that', do you?!"

I said: "What do you mean, *Industria*?"

"At the *Industria*, your car will have its technical examination."

140

I'd half expected this, but no-one had mentioned it before. "Where is the *Industría*?"

"In Badalona, señor. Here is a map. We shall call you."

Before I left, I had to pay my dues to El Rack, totalling about a zillion pesetas, or £650 in real money. Also before I left, I took my Spanish plates – green or not – and went upstairs at El Rack to insure Sutty. This procedure, apart from some confusion about some "crystals", went pretty smoothly. If only El Rack's insurance desk ran the Jesters' department as well.

Sutty was insured on the strength of the temporary green licence plates for a whole year. As a gesture of defiance, though, I never bothered actually putting the plates on the car, and ten years and another country later they sit outside in my shed, gathering dust but still pristinely unriveted.

A few more days passed. Another call. "Señor Geesay, you have your appointment at the *Industría*. You must go to Badalona tomorrow morning at the nines. Do you understand, señor?"

"Yes, yes, Badalona at the nines. Adiós."

Now, I was a little concerned about this technical exam. Sutty was perfectly roadworthy, all his lights worked and so on. But his headlights pointed to the right only because of those nifty black stickers which I'd stuck on in the scented hills above Grasse in some other lifetime. The *Contrôle de Sécurité* in Grenoble had been perfectly happy about them, but the *Industría* in Badalona ...?

I pulled into the queue of cars at the garage, for this is what it was. (I never discovered why it's called the *Industría*.) I got out and went up to the office with my papers.

"I'm here for the technical examination, so my English car can have its Spanish plates."

"You must first do the importation of the car."

(Gott in Himmel!) "Tranquillo. El Rack has done all that."

"Oh, El Rack!" The minion sprung to attention. "You will follow me, please, señor." I was impressed – El Rack must be a good customer. Down one or two passages and into another office. He showed me to a smartly dressed official behind a desk. "This is Señor Rack, señor", he said, and left us.

Señor Rack (a remarkable coincidence of surname) had me move Sutty from the ragged line of old bangers where I'd left him, to a much more disciplined and shorter line nearby.

I sat at the wheel for about five minutes. Señor Rack then started marching down the line of his charges, collecting papers from their drivers. As he came to Sutty, of course, he had to weave across to the other side of the line, to my side of the car. As he did so, his gait slowed and his expression changed for the worse. He looked at me through the windscreen, pointed at the steering wheel and proceeded to wag his forefinger in that most negative manner favoured by the Catalans. Señor Rack approached my window.

"Es imposibile, señor."

"What's impossible?"

"In Spain, you cannot matriculate a car with the steering wheel here on the right. Is illegal, señor."

It must have been a delayed reaction to the continual exposure to all these jesters, but I'm afraid I burst out laughing. Señor Rack seemed gravely disappointed at this reaction.

"Is true, señor. Is impossible.

"It's possible in France."

"This is not France, señor."

I could not deny it. "So what can I do?"

"You could move the wheel, señor."

(I really must look up the Spanish for buffoon.)

"Er, and the pedals and the dashboard?", I suggested.

"Is possible, señor."

This is a seven-year-old Corolla, not a Bentley!

"Señor should go to the office of El Rack. It is at Santalo ..."

"I know where is El Rack, Señor Rack. I spend there my holidays. Gracias."

And with that, I pulled out of the line and onto the road. As I headed back through the grey streets of Badalona, it gradually dawned on me that this was indescribably perfect! The only reason I'd wanted the Spanish registration was to get Sutty insured. Sutty was now insured, but I couldn't register the car. I'd claim my money back from El Rack and drive around forever with my French plates, like any other "tourist". *La vie en rose!* I pulled up at a Badalona bar for a Badalona beer.

More Spaniards in the Works

For a few months, Sutty and I loitered lazily in this twighlight zone between registrations. We had to adjust our plans slightly. The French plates tended to cause occasional hassles over the border in France, where the gendarmes naturally expected a car with French plates to have a *vignette* – French tax disc. When they stopped me and demanded an explanation, my combination of French plates, Spanish insurance, Spanish resident's permit, French or British registration document and Spanish or British driving licence, had them waving me away with an "Allez-y, m'sieur, c'est trop compliqué!" So, to avoid this continuous delay, I gave Sutty back his British plates. Now I looked like a simple British tourist in both Spain and France, unless anyone bothered to notice the "F" for France and the 'El RACC' stickers incongruously placed above the British registration number.

Then, true to form, El Rack tried to put one or two more Spaniards in the works. My rather brilliant letter[46] claiming back my zillion pesetas pointed out that a motoring organization might reasonably be expected to know where to find the steering wheel on a British car. The *bufonas*[47] replied, claiming that they didn't know it was a British car, as it had been imported from France. Needless to say, by return of post they received a copy of my magnificent A4 summary of Sutty's history, with a reminder that I twice offered this concise document to their incompetent staff, only to have them hand it back; "Perhaps it would finally be of some help to their investigations ...?"

Their next move was about two months later when they called me at my office. At first, I understood very little that the young woman at the other end of the line was saying – she seemed to be using one of the 18 tenses of Spanish which I had not yet covered with Esther – and so I asked my Catalan colleague Jaume to deal with her. He took

---

[46] Well, all right, my teacher's brilliant letter, which toned down to an acceptable Spanish level my rather acid English pen. In fact, she deleted everything I'd written and started from scratch.

[47] I'll have to invent the word - it's not in the dictionary - no wonder Hancock waon't very hig over here.

the receiver, listened intently, nodded verbally and put the receiver down.

"What's the news, Jaume?"

"She says it may still be possible to register a British car in Spain, and she'll call you back."

"Thanks. I didn't understand a word she was saying."

"I'm not surprised. She was using many conditional and subjunctive tenses."

"Does this mean there's some doubt to her claim?"

"A big amount of doubt, Ricardo."

Sutty in Trouble

Things were quiet for a while. I drove around with my miscellaneous bundle of documents and number plates, minding my own business. El Rack ignored me and so, fortunately, did the local constabulary.

Then one day El Rack arose from its slumbers to call me.

"Señor Guise, we have found the solution! You can register your car, but you need un espejo."

Espejo. I know this word. *Espejo, espejo en la pared* ...yes – a mirror! They're saying I need a mirror!

"Señor Guise, are you still there?"

"Yes, I'm here. My car already has several mirrors."

"You need a special mirror, señor. You must come into the office of El Rack. It's on Santaló ..."

"I know where El Rack is. I'll come in tomorrow."

So, another half-day off work. It was autumn again, over a year since I first wandered nonchalantly down Carrer Santaló. In comparison with these guys, the Poncets of Grenoble had been positively oiling the wheels of a sleek administrative machine. Anyway, maybe Sutty would soon be registered after all. Inside El Rack, the Jesters' Desk had moved, but the face behind it was familar – the woman who foolishly rejected my A4 Potted History of Sutty.

"Buenas dias. I am Señor Guise. You have information for me on a special mirror I need in order to register my English car in Spain."

"Yes, Señor Guise. You have the mirror?"

144

"Que?! I come here to learn information on the mirror. Which kind of special mirror?"

"Well, a special mirror for cars with the steering wheel on the right, when the steering wheel should be on the left. You should know – you are English, no?"

"I am English, yes, but in England the steering wheel should not be on the left. I know nothing of this special mirror. Where can I buy it?"

"Well, in England of course, señor!"

My death ray stare inexplicably failed to evaporate her on the spot. I spoke calmly: "I live here in Barcelona. That is why I wish to register my car in Barcelona. I do not live in England. I do not shop in England. You are El Rack. Can you not obtain for me this special mirror?"

"I'm sorry, señor. We are El Rack. We have no business with England."

So the sole thing we were agreed upon was that they were El Rack. They were also el incompetent time-wasters who had just cost me another half-day off work on a wild mirror chase. This *bufona* standing in front of me clearly thought that, being English, I was in constant telepathic contact with all things English and could beam the special mirror across the Channel directly on to my English car.

"By chance, I shall visit England next month", I informed her. "I shall investigate and return. Good day."

The Wild Goose and the Windy Day

December in Long Eaton always was bleak and grey; December 1993 was also windy and wet. I dived out of the weather into the motor accessories shop on Main Street and pulled back my wet hood, instantly steaming up my glasses. I felt my way to the counter.

"Hello. I'm looking for a mirror for right-hand-drive cars to drive on the Continent."

"Ah, you lucky bugger, off to the sun, eh? What kind of mirror?"

I had feared this question.

"I don't know. Is there a standard one?"

"No idea, mate. Anyhow, we ain't got nuthin' for the continent. You wanna try the big boys: Halfords might know."

145

A blustery drive in the hire car to the nearest Halfords, on a wind-swept industrial estate that had appeared since Sutty and I had left for the sun five years previously. This time the assistant had actually heard about mirrors for the Continent.

"Yes, a couple of months ago, some bloke who was off to France for his hols came in here asking about mirrors. Or was that caravan mirrors? Any road, it was something about mirrors, I'm sure."

"Er, what did you sell him?"

"Oh, we didn't know what he was on about." This was looking more and more like a wild goose chase. "So we sent him to the RAC."

Brilliant, the Royal Automobile Club! The Rack!! Why didn't I think of that? Maybe the club that doesn't need to say what country it's from knows more than its incompetent Catalan cousin. I dived once more into the elements and headed for the same RAC office where I'd bought Sutty's yellow and black shades five years before. It was Saturday lunchtime and already getting dark. I pulled into the car park outside the RAC, just as its lights were being dimmed. Oh no, Saturday afternoon closing! Feeing sure the secret of the mirror was in there, I leapt from the car and into the office. A young woman approached me.

"We're just closing, sir."

"I've come all the way from Barcelona. You must help me." My accent sounded more like Beeston than Barcelona. She raised an eyebrow.

"I need a mirror for driving on the Continent. It's urgent."

"Mr Nixon deals with Continental Motoring. I'll see if he's still here."

She disappeared. Continental Motoring! They admitted that the rest of the world exists! I was definitely on to something here. From behind the map shelves emerged a tall man, already wrapped up in hat and scarf to brave the weather en route home.

"You're going abroad, sir?"

"I'm already there."

He didn't seem convinced.

"Er, I mean I already live there and my car has a right-hand drive and theirs don't, well naturally they don't I mean, and I need a mirror to register the car, a special mirror, special for the Continent you see, and ..."

He held up his hand.

"You need a mirror to aid visibility for Continental Motoring, sir."

Sense at last. "Exactly. Do they exist?"

"Yes, sir."

Brilliant. "Can I buy one?"

"No, sir."

Aaaaaargh. "Why not?"

"It's December, sir. There's no demand."

I couldn't think of anything to say.

"It's the weather, you see," he continued. "People don't go to Europe in December. We'll have them in stock at Easter."

I thought of reminding him that we were already standing in Europe and that the winter in Spain was most agreeable, but didn't see much point.

"Will there be anything else, sir? No? Then, good day, and enjoy your trip."

He left, and I trudged out after him, defeated. Sutty's insurance would run out well before I could even get a sniff of the magic mirror, and my hopes of getting him re-insured were not high. I popped into the pub next door and tried to formulate a plan over a pint. The only plan I could think of was to have another pint.

Sutty Goes Home

Without the magic mirror, Sutty was doomed.

The fact that I could and did drive him around Barcelona with perfect visibility didn't matter. In a few weeks his insurance on the temporary registration would run out, and as a combination Sutty and I were uninsurable. Catch *veíntidos*, remember.

Back in Spain again, I called a few British insurance companies, just in case some part of the European Union had finally realized that motorists exist beyond their borders and are just queuing up to be insured. But no, I'm afraid to report that we still had (and probably have) a long way to go.

"Hello, I'd like a quote for car insurance please."

Norwich Union: "Your name and address, sir?"

"My name is Guise. The address is in Spain – should I spell it?"

Silence.

"Hello?"

"Er, when are you going to Spain, sir?"

"I'm already there. I'm calling from Spain."

I might as well have said I was a gaseous life form transmitting my voice-like signals from the doomed planet Vzog.

"Er. Mmmm. We don't deal with that kind of thing, sir."

That kind of thing?! The Egyptian tablet manufacturer probably said the same when Caxton offered him the African franchise for his paperbacks.

I tried the Co-op. After all, I'd been a customer of theirs for a good many years before finding life beyond Dover. The local agent in Nottingham actually knew my name. Things were getting off to a good start. If I said I was a British resident and gave him a British address, he'd be prepared to believe me. Then it transpired that I'd have to sign the forms in his presence. Not wanting to fund a weekend away for him in sunny Spain, I declined.

And so, one grey day in January 1994, Sutty's insurance finally expired. For a few weeks we still drove around as though nothing had changed, but eventually friends persuaded me that this was madness. Good name for a compilation album, I thought, and, humming *Baggy Trousers*, trundled Sutty into the office car park. The firm's friendly car park rep believed my story that it was all the firm's fault and let me leave Sutty there until I could get him back to England, without sending me nasty messages in Catalan about the misuse of company property.

So Sutty sat out the winter and I let the train take the strain. Sutty sat out the spring and I started to envisage the sweaty trips on the 1715 from Sant Cugat, wedged for forty minutes next to a large, brown Catalan woman with a large, black fan.

In June I took the plunge and bought a Spanish car. Five years of stout resistence to the demon left-hand drives finally collapsed, in the form of a rusty 12-year-old Renault 9, with squishy seats, no screen washer and – periodically – no lights. It had the acceleration of a wheezy mule and, from its BFK initials, was christened Beefcake. In the car park, I introduced Beefcake to Sutty, who simply sulked under his layer of Spanish dust.

Then, one bright morning in July, an old friend in England called to admit he was going to let the side down and get married, and that he thought his only chance of being dissuaded was by me, over a pint, the night before the sinister ceremony. If I could make it, I'd be invited to the wedding too. Something told me he was not over-confident in my powers of dissuasion.

This sounded like the chance Sutty was waiting for: escape back to civilisation. I had three months to try and figure out how to get him back to Blighty without any papers.

1. I could dig a tunnel from the Sant Cugat car park to the White Cliffs of Dover. Well, if I had to choose anywhere in Europe to hide three million cubic metres of dirt, Barcelona wouldn't be a bad choice. Certainly no-one would bat an eyelid if, everytime I stood at a bar, I dropped a few piles of dubious-looking substance out of the bottom of my trousers. (If you haven't been in a typical Barcelona bar, you'll just have to take my word for this.) No, I'd run out of petrol somewhere below the Massif Central.

2. I could drive at top-speed across the countryside, leaping – Steve-McQueen-like – straight across ravines, and crashing – James-Bond-like – straight through the crash barriers at the frontier posts, waving my big blue British passport. No, Sutty's not very good in the rough.

3. I could avoid France altogether and drive very carefully and anonymously to a Northern Spanish port and there catch a ferry to England. Mmm, this sounded more like it. Why didn't Donald Pleasance think of that?

So I found a slightly more enlightened British insurance company which was prepared to believe that I existed simply by dint of my having a voice on the phone and my despatching some dosh through the post. They agreed to insure Sutty from midnight on the day of his return to the green and pleasant land – in the form of Portsmouth harbour – and didn't want to know how, or from where, he got there. The only question left now was how to keep a low profile en route to and in Bilbao.

I managed the 'en route' easily enough by ignoring the *autopistas.*, where the danger areas would have been the toll booths. I could imagine one of the tollsters speaking to me normally in Spanish, und then, just as I was about to pull away, whispering "Good luck, mate" in English. I'd nod, say "Thanks, mate" and suddenly find half the Spanish Gestapo at the window and a machine gun up my nostril. So instead Sutty and I spent 12 hours bumbling anonymously along the by-ways of Aragon and Navarra, and a very pleasant bumble it was too.

I solved the 'in Bilbao' by not going there. *Ach, fiendish Englische Schweinhund!* Just in case old Larry 'Ludwig' Blenkinsop had been the Jerry spy we always suspected, and the Hun had tipped off Interpol to search the Bilbao hotels, I took a right in the twighlight at Pamplona, before diving down the Pyrenean foothills to San Sebastian. There I found an innocent-looking seafront hotel with an underground garage, where I stashed Sutty out of sight for three days.

Sutty's last day on foreign soil dawned cool and misty. We chugged up the ramp from his bolthole and this time made straight for the *autopista.* No point in getting lost at this stage. The friendly fog shrouded our gentle, hour-long run through the Basque Country, as we skirted Bilbao and pulled into the ferry terminal.

The man on the gate was too interested in my tickets and passport to notice the mysterious absence of stickers on Sutty's windscreen. So was the man who ushered us into the queue on the dock. By a stroke of luck, we found ourselves between a splendid, green, British-registered Morgan and a Spanish car whose occupants were involved in a loud argument about cabins. Both easily drew attention away from my innocent little Toyota.

Despite all the ballyhoo in the papers, there were still customs and police checkpoints in the EU. At least there were at Bilbao, presumably to wish ETA terrorists *buen viaje* on their shopping holidays to the Bomb-It-All megastore in Kilburn.

The checkpoint was just before the ramp onto the ferry, where the sun glistened on the windows of the empty booths. The Gestapo were all outside, swarming around the vehicles as they passed slowly through. Would they notice the mismatch between Sutty's British plates and the blank windscreen? All my plans were based on the assumption that no-one would look for this until I was entering Britain.

Following the Morgan, I approached in a confident third gear, but sweat trickled down my brow. In sight was the ramp to freedom. I felt my heart beating against my Aberystwyth sweatshirt. The contingent on our lane was two green-uniformed policemen with guns slung over their shoulders and three unarmed customs officials in black. One of the customs men waved down the Morgan. I slowed to second. A bead of sweat slid into my right eye. The taller policeman waved me to pull past the Morgan. I nonchalantly threw my passport onto the top of the dashboard and scratched my nose. The policeman looked through the windscreen and reached for his gun. I briefly wondered if I'd make it up the ramp if I put my foot down and crouched low in the hail of bullets. He hitched his gun higher on his shoulder, scratched his ear and walked straight past Sutty to get a better look at the back of the Morgan. Foot steady, Sutty still in second, we bounced onto the ramp, up the ramp, off the ramp and into the cool black safety of the car deck. Into position, engine off.

I sat still for a while as cars bumped up behind me. Eventually, tapping the centre of the steering wheel, I muttered "We made it, Sutts."

Bazzaranshaz

We made it at Portsmouth too. I'd attached to the windscreen a circular sticker that would have held the tax disc if I had one. Instead I wrote a little note announcing our arrival back home and saying that I'd get my MOT and therefore my tax disc at the first opportunity, i.e. Monday morning. I don't know whether anyone read it, but nobody stopped us.

Monday morning saw Sutty and me at the Derby Road Service Station, Long Eaton. Relieved at last to be able to get things done in my native language, I confidently sauntered up to the reception desk and pinged the oily bell, whereupon an oily youth emerged from the workshop.

"Ayup."[48]

---

[48] For the benefit of foreigners (i.e. anyone from beyond Kegworth) translations appear on page 155.

"Hello", I said, "I'd like to book my Toyota in for an MOT as early as possible today please."

"Tharritaahthaya?"

My Long Eaton dialect must have been a bit rusty. I understood him less than either the Poncets of Grenoble or the Jesters of Barcelona.

"Er, sorry?"

"Tharri?" he repeated, pointing at Sutty out on the forecourt.

"Ah, yes, that's it."

"Yagorranowdun?"

My ear[49] was gradually attuning. "An old what?"

"Yerowd emmowtay. Seizure wivviowdun."

"Well, the last MOT's five years old. The latest I've got's in French, if that's any use?" A stupid question, if ever there was one.

"Bludjell! Jeertha', Shaz?" He was shouting to his mate in the workshop. "Juwannan emmowtay in bluddifrog?" Shaz's position on the linguistic proposal was unclear. His colleague snorted and, looking at me through knowing oily eyes, said in a low voice, "Owd Shaz cunardliray dinglish, lerralownowtelse. Amva brayans rahndeer." He thought this was hilarious and snorted loudly, while I thought it best to keep a straight face.

"Rightoguv, levitwiyus 'ngizzabuzz arahntow. Eskfubazza."

I got all this first time and left. "Pretty soon I'll be speaking like a native", I thought. "Wait a minute, I am a native." I was just on my way across the forecourt when Bazza called me back.

"Ayup, ayagenuzkayz?"

"I got the last syllable: keys. "Oh, they're in the car.", I said. Then, deciding I may as well dip my toe in to test the water, I ventured: "Traa!"

"Traamay'."

Ha, acceptance! What a strange feeling, after five years of listening to Grenoblois and Catalan. I wandered back across the park practising my conjugations:

---

[49] Did I tell you I only had one ear?

Tugiyi' (to give it)
ah giyi'
yo genni'
ay gizi'
way gizi'
yowlo' gizi'
thi' giyi'

Eezipeezi!

I called at two as instructed. A grunt at the other end.

"Hello, is that Bazza?"

Another grunt, then silence. Then: "Bazzarrhoea." Better than diarrhoea, I suppose. The grunt must have been the enigmatic Shaz.

"It's Mr Guise here, about my car."

"Oyeh. Yuddun, mate. Cumrahn wenyalayak."

I liked straight away. Now, to a technical dunce like me, the bit when the motor mechanic tells you what he had to do to your car is so far above my head that it may as well be on the surface of Pluto, and so what language it comes in is irrelevant. English, French, Spanish, Catalan – I've heard them all and am none the wiser. Still, to stand and listen to it seems to be a duty you can't avoid, like school assembly. I stood to attention as Bazza went through the hymnsheet.

"Well fustup, yuwales wuz raytaaht. Widdida lorrarajusmanz 'nnah thizballunst. Yupadz wuzonthi lasslegz sowipurron noounz, 'nyublayadz wudoji 'nsowiddidum tbeeyonsefsahd. Yufrun'tredz uzwossnbakuns, bu'yukan jussabah' gerrawaywiyi'. Nowtelswurrup."

I thought he'd finished, so I nodded wisely and said, "I see. Er, how much does it come to?"

"Including the MOT, that will be one hundred and thirty-two pounds exactly, sir."

Nice one, Bazza.

And so I took my bright new MOT certificate down to the Post Office, where I purchased a bright new tax disc to last into 1995. With his tax disc installed proudly in the windscreen, Sutty was suddenly legal: insured, MOT'd and taxed. What I'd failed to do in two years in Spain took less than twenty-four hours in Britain.

I'd no time to advertise him for sale, and so when I went back to the Continent a few days later, Sutty stayed locked up in midad's garage, no doubt sulking at the injustice of it all. After a five-year tour of duty under the punishing Mediterranean sun, consigned to rust away in the cold and the damp. Is this a home fit for heroes?

A Long Eatonian – English Glossary

Long Eatonian	English
Ayup	Hello
Tharri?	Is that it?
Tharritaahthaya?	Is that it out there?
Yagorranowdun?	Have you got an old one?
Yerowd emmowtay. Seizure wivviowdun.	Your old MOT. It's easier with the old one.
Bludjell! Jeertha', Shaz? Juwannan emmowtay in bluddifrog? Owd Shaz cunardliray dinglish, lerralownowtelse. Amva brayans rahndeer	Gosh! Did you hear that, Charles? Do you want an MOT in French? Dear old Charles can hardly read English, let alone anything else. I'm the brains around here.
Rightoguv, levitwiyus 'ngizzabuzz arahntow. Eskfubazza	Jolly good, sir. Leave it with us and phone at about two o'clock. Ask for Barry.
Ayup, ayagenuzkayz	I say, have you given us the keys?
Traa!	Cheerio!
Traamay'!	Cheerio, old man!
Eezipeezi!	Really quite easy!
Bazzarrhoca	Barry speaking
Oyeh. Yuddun, mate. Cumrahn wenyalayak	Ah yes. We've finished it, old man. Come round whenever you like.

cont'd...

cont'd...

Long Eatonian	English
Well fustup, yuwales wuz raytaaht. Widdida lorrarajusmanz 'nnah thizballunst. Yupadz wuzonthi lasslegz sowipurron noounz, 'nyublayadz wudoji 'nsowiddidum tbeeyonsefsahd. Yufrun'tredz uzwossnbakuns, bu'yukan jussabah' gerrawaywiyi'. Nowtelswurrup.	Well, to start with, your wheels were completely misaligned. We made many adjustments and now they're balanced. Your brake pads were in rather poor condition, so we installed new ones; and your wiper blades were imperfect, so we replaced them to be on the safe side. The treads on the front wheels are worse than those on the back, but you'd just survive a police inspection. Nothing else was amiss.
Including the MOT, that will be one hundred and thirty-two pounds exactly, sir.	Including the MOT, that will be one hundred and thirty-two pounds exactly, sir.

14. Sutty sports his recently acquired French plates on a jaunt in the Alpes Maritimes. The last two digits of French registrations indicate the department: 38 is Isere. 1990. *Photo: author*

15. Everything seemed to be happening at once in Barcelona in 1992. This is the Olympic Stadium two weeks after the Olympic Games, when the Paralympics drew huge crowds. *Photo: author*

16. After F.C. Barcelona's Camp Nou stadium, every other football arena seems like Grange Park. Cruyff's Barca won the European Cup in 1992. The following year, this capcity crowd of around 125,000 saw them beat the 'other' Barcelona side, Espanyol, 4-0 in a league match. *Photo: author*

8

Bungling for Boys

Continental Ear

The traditional Englishman's attitude to foreign languages goes something like "Well, I can order a beer in most languages – *oon bee-air sivouplay; oona serv-acer porfevor* – and that's all you need, in't it?" Well, yes, except that's not how they actually order a beer in France or Spain... any more than "A beer, please" is how you order a pint of bitter in an English pub – unless you're American, in which case you slam a 'Gimme' on the front for good measure. And drop the 'please.'

What I'm getting at in a roundabout way is that, if you want to fit in your local like a local (and, I admit, there's no particular reason why you should), you need to listen to your actual foreigners ordering their beers before you boast about your skills to your mates back home. I know this because, to my enduring regret, I never really got the hang of it in seven years on the Continent – and I'm tempted to put this failure down Continental Ear.

What the French actually ask for is 'une pression' and they get a draft beer. I listened to them saying it at the admirable Tonneau Bar in Grenoble's Place Notre Dame for, I would say, about 850 evenings. But when *I* asked for "Une pression, s'il vous plaît", what I generally got was a blank look and a "Monsieur?"

"Une pression, s'il vous plaît", I repeated, very slowly and with impressive Gallic reverberation on the 'r'.

"Fanta de citron, monsieur?"

"Non, une p r e s s i o n."

"??"

161

"Une bière!"

"Ah, une pression, monsieur! Ba, ouai!"

I never discovered what it was in my careful intonation that didn't quite match the waiter's aural expectations, but I do know that Continental Ear is also rife in Spain. We English are so used to hearing our own language murdered by the Anglically-challenged from remotest China, California or Chelmsford that we've developed an automatic filter mechanism that figures out the essence of the words we hear from the strangled accompaniments. The rest of the world expects to hear its own language used perfectly and, lacking the English filter, therefore suffers from Continental Ear. That's my theory.

The best example I know from Spain is not my own battle with the waiter at Sant Cugat's equally admirable Mesón, who had great difficulty in believing that my nightly request for "un tubo", which echoed the self-same request by every other customer, was not an order for a sack of pink aubergines, but is from a James Faulkner (he of the compass and bamboo thicket).

Jim was, and is, a talented linguist whose grasp of not just the vocabulary but also the tenor of a new language was disconcertingly rapid. However, one day in the Barcelona suburbs, when in search of the nearest railway station, he hailed a passing Catalan gentleman and asked directions to "Los Ferrocarriles de Catalunya?" (Local stations in Barcelona are referred to by the railway company they serve.)

"Señor?"

"Dónde está la estación de Los Ferrocarriles de Catalunya, por favor, señor?"

"Los que?"

"F e r r o c a r r i l e s   d e   C a t a l u n y a!"

A short silence followed, after which the bemused gentleman ventured:

"Un buzón?"

???!!!

Now, even in English the nearest railway station doesn't sound remotely like a postbox. You see, it's not just me.

The Man With No Name

One or two of my little misunderstandings may have been down to my own errors, though. I admit it was probably my fault that my Spanish next-door neighbour always hid behind her door after our first meeting, when, instead of greeting her with "Soy encantado, señora" (I'm pleased to meet you), I inadvertently came out with "Soy un cortado, señora" (I'm a small, white coffee).

My attempt to get a telephone in Spain was also rather bungled.

Having recently arrived from a three-year stint in France, my little brain cell devoted to foreign languages was naturally full of French, where 'nombre' means number. This explains why, when the receptionist at the local Telefónica office asked me "Su nombre, por favor, señor?" (Your name, please, sir?), I automatically replied:

"No tengo un nombre" (I have no name). After all, most of the customers here would have already had a phone number in Spain. My reply, however, was clearly not what she was expecting. She looked doubtful:

"No tiene un nombre?"

"No. Acabo de llegar en España y no tengo un nombre." (I've just arrived in Spain and have no name.)

After an uncomfortable delay, she saw an ingenious way around this unexpected problem: "Pues, que es el nombre de su padre?" (What's your father's name?)

Not seeing the relevance, but keen to help, I told her: "972 3332."

This was too much. With a lengthening queue behind me, the receptionist pointed to an isolated chair in the corner of the room and asked me sternly to "Espere alli, por favor, señor!"

For the next hour, all the customers before me in the queue, and then all those after me, were duly called by name and ushered to a desk, there doubtless to be granted their new telephones. During this time, I imagine, worried committees had been meeting out of public view in an effort to figure out how to enter in their directories a subscriber with no name. Eventually, when the rest of the room had been empty for a long five minutes, and I was still sitting patiently on my little chair in the corner, the Telefónica representative who'd drawn the short straw approached me with a hesitant step.

"Er, el hombre sin nombre?" (The man with no name?)

In fact, I have also to admit that this was actually my second attempt just to get into the Telefónica building. The first time it had been unexpectedly locked up and in darkness, and a helpful passer-by had explained the reason to me. I looked it up in my dictionary. On my return to my office, our secretary asked if I'd got my new phone.

"No, I'm afraid not."

"But you've been away for over an hour. What's the problem?"

"The Telefónica office is closed, Elisa."

"But why? It's normally open at this time."

She dragged it out of me. "Well, apparently it's closed due to a sudden area of market gardening around Seville."

And I'll let you Spanish-speakers work that one out for yourself.

The Long-Running Affair, Episode 6

Oddly enough, despite all my bungled attempts at communication outside the office, I was making some kind of contribution within it. This was probably because the company that had so generously offered me an escape route from England was in fact American and therefore, even though they used far too many syllables, at least the words they formed were a kind of English. The products I was to work on were, however, all Greek to me.

People say that we never notice a revolution till it's over. Which people? Well, I don't know. In fact, I just made that up, but it sounds reasonable, doesn't it? The very office where I worked for three years in Grenoble was at the heart of a very particular computer revolution – and even then it didn't dawn on me till years later what was actually going on.

Before I started the job, while Sutty and I (and others) were on holiday in Grasse that summer of '89, I swotted up computer networks under the fig trees with the help of many a *kir royal* and a big red book I'd bought called, conveniently, 'Computer Networks'. It was heavy stuff, I can tell you: LANs, WANs, synchronicity, asynchronicity, X.25, X.33, the X99 to Birmingham, calling at Ashby-de-la-Zouch... my little head was reeling even before I started.

On my first day, after having been initiated, de-loused and hosed down, a nice young chap showed me to my desk, which was completely bare save for a white note from my new boss, telling me that he was in hospital and that if I didn't know much about computer networks (good guess), I should sign up for a two-week course in Brussels, all expenses paid. So this was what multinational corporations did! I liked it, Captain Mainwaring, I liked it. Naturally I despatched myself to Brussels without delay and there learnt a lot more about LANs, WANs, synchronicity, asynchronicity, X.25, X.33 and the X98 to a very strange disco somewhere behind the Grand' Place.

Duly swotted up, I was allocated to a team developing a nifty little device called an X.25/84 Multiplexer. My job was to write a manual telling people how to use it, which should have been a piece of cake – after all, I'd been writing computer manuals for years, I'd spent the best part of the last month learning about networks and I was surrounded by bright and talented engineers who ate, drank and slept multiplexers. My only problem was that I didn't actually grasp – in the sense of understand on a fairly basic sort of level – what on earth a multiplexer was.

I therefore ordered one and it arrived on my desk. It was grey and square, with lots of big sockets in the back (at least I assumed that was the back) and a few lights on the front. It had a kind of little keypad and a kind of little screen, and when you switched it on it said "@".

OK, I'll get straight to the point here. Some years later, a dim little dawning in my dim little head told me that what these guys were doing with their mysterious grey boxes in that featureless grey building in a Grenoble suburb in 1989 was in fact constructing the nuts and bolts of the Internet. That multiplexer was a Web server, except that there was very little Web to serve at the time, unless you were a professor of astrophysics at Cornell. I wrote the goddam' manual for the thing and I *still* couldn't see the revolution that was happening right there under my nose. Literally. Ain't that a darn thing?

My American English was coming along fine, though. My Chinese however was poor, but this didn't stop the company twice sending me to the Far East on missions whose purpose I now forget, but whose crazy luxuries will probably linger in a guilty memory for ever. This is the story of just the first day of the the first trip... if you count a day as being from sleep to sleep.

The Rongest Day

It was the dream business trip. Two weeks in the Orient, with a schedule that shows only four days actual work. Ten years before I would have given if not exactly my right arm for this trip, then at least all my right sleeves. As it happened, this chance of a lifetime arrived at a point when a weekend jetting off to foreign parts might just be outweighed on the scales of pleasure to a weekend resting my own parts on the sofa, with a good book and a passable beer. That's what a year of over-travel does for you. The company seemed strangely keen to send its employees to all points of the compass on any excuse. That training course in Brussels was just the start; by the time I'd been transferred to Barcelona, my sturdy blue passport was getting distinctly dog-eared... and then the travelling doubled.

But China! Hong Kong!! Taiwan and maybe Macau!!! I forced myself to think with exclamation marks and despatched myself to a travel bookshop. The Librería Francesa, the 'French Bookshop' in Barcelona, actually sells English travel books. Fiendishly inscrutable, these Spaniards. (Still trying to get myself in the mood.) I came away with Berlitz's *China* (plus Plaza and Jané's map), The Lonely Planet's *Taiwan*, and *The Rough Guide to Hong Kong and Macau*. Only *The Rough Guide* eventually became as happily dog-eared as my passport. I settled down to an evening's swotting, flicking, poring and finally, after seeing off the best part of a bottle of Penèdes, simply musing. OK, the travel bug had been duly re-injected and I was in the mood – and spiritually ready to go.

Two weeks and 40 hours of overtime later, I was also more or less physically ready to go.

From Heaven to Hell

Saturday morning. Barcelona - Zurich on Swissair. I'd never flown Swissair. Indeed, I'd always pooh-poohed the idea that there's anything to choose between one airline and the next, seeing that kind of thing as just a piece of middle-class travelmanship, a subject raised just to prove what a jet-setter you are. I mean, they just give you a seat, take off, give you some food and then land – they're all the same, aren't they? Five minutes into the 08:35 to Zurich and I'd finally seen the light. Swissair was streets, or rather flight paths, above the rest[50]. I was later to find that the other end of the spectrum was occupied by the appropriately named Dragonair – after 35 years of flying the middle ground, I flew the two extremes in the space of a day.

Why was Swissair so good? Well, it sounds a cliché, but I really felt they treated me as an individual. Although I was in Economy (I'd never flown anything else), the First Class stewardess spotted my 'Boise Idaho' T-shirt and came down amongst the plebs to tell me that she'd spent some time there and what had I been doing there? She spoke to me in a heavily accented Spanish, but, taking her to be Swiss German, I replied in German and she actually understood me. (You have to have heard my dreadful German to understand how hard that must have been.) The Economy stewardess then came around with free newspapers. Nothing unusual in that, but the English paper was not the usual inexplicable choice between two extremes, *The Financial Times* and *The Mail*, but was instead *The Independent*. What luxury! A 30-minute delay in takeoff and automatically an orange juice. Swissair just did it better, that's all.

Still Saturday morning. Zurich International Airport. We'd obviously crossed the border into Northern Europe: neat fields and detached houses, a gaggle of plane-spotters at the end of the runway, a calmly efficient transit lounge. In Spain, this lounge would be a smoking mass of litter-louts; in the U.S., there'd be the standard proportion (is it 10%?) of loudly complaining 'customers' bitching about the lack of service. There was, however, a noisy English family trying to eat a snack out of plastic bags – thermos flask of milky coffee, jam sandwiches in cellophane, and a Swiss roll (ha ha). Clearly Continental cooking was still deeply suspect and to be avoided at all costs. Unlike their headgear it seemed: Dad was wearing a Swiss-style felt hat complete with feathers. Their young son was showing more interest in the display of electronic games than in the sticky snack prepared by his mother: "Timothy, I'm going to smack you *very hard!*" After some time abroad, you take more notice of English people... and it's usually a less than uplifting experience.

Saturday afternoon. Zurich - Hong Kong on Cathay Pacific. Now, a recent revelation to me was that you can reserve your seat on a

---

[50] Which makes it rather a shame that it was to disappear from the skies altogether some eight years later.

167

plane before you get to the airport! You worldly-wise folks probably knew that all along, but no booking agent had ever offered me the chance and so I'd no reason to know. I admit I'd always wondered why, even when I turned up at the airport hours before take-off expressly to get a window seat, it was still possible that they'd all gone... just how early do these people turn up?! Well, earlier that year, while flying around the U.S., where they treat air travel like the rest of the world treats train travel (and, perversely, treat train travel like the rest of the world treats air travel), I'd learned a few tricks. So when I booked my outward flight to Hong Kong I got in early with my standard window-non-smoking preference and so was actually looking forward to this 12-hour marathon, as we should be passing over some fascinating terrain. Indeed we did: Poland, Moscow, Tashkent, Pakistan, the northern plain of India, Calcutta, Thailand, and southern China. I know this because they all came up on that brilliant invention, newly arrived at the time – the multi-scaled route map displayed on the movie screen. And how much of this rolling Eurasian panorama did I see? None at all, that's how much. Zippo. My 'window' seat turned out to be a wall seat. There *was* a window a little way behind me, and another a little way in front, but even when I stood up and gawped annoyingly over the heads of my fore- and aft-neighbours, all I saw was wing. And beneath that wing was the Gobi Desert. Next time I'd specify "window-next-to-the-seat-with-view-not-of-wing-non-smoking".

The less said about those uncomfortable 13 hours the better. Yes, we were late as well. Not a wink of sleep, as the plane was full and I can't sleep vertically. At least I didn't miss the fabled spectacle of landing at Hong Kong's Tai Pak Airport[51], since there was nothing to be seen but mist and rain. The British pilot warned us it would be a little "bumpy" before touchdown. What he might have added, but wisely chose not to, was that we'd be landing in a typhoon.

It was ten hours later that I discovered that the bumpy conditions had a name and it was Typhoon Dot: the headline news on BBC World Service in Asia, and we were in the middle of it. We landed, skidded about a bit and then the pilot apologized for "parking" near the hangars, but explained that we'd got to wait a while for a proper

---

[51] Since replaced by Chek Lap Kok airport, where the wing-tips of landing Jumbos finally clear the windows of the downtown tower blocks by considerably more than ten feet.

parking slot. Very quick thinking that. He could have said "Sorry we're out here at the edge of the airport – at least we came to a standstill before I tipped the old crate into the South China Sea! Ha ha!", but wisely didn't. (This is exactly what happened five days later in another typhoon, when a similar 747 of China Airlines, did skid halfway into the sea.)

The worst was yet to come, in the form of Dragonair – the Far East's equivalent of the Red Arrows, except that the oriental version does its acts of bravado with passengers on board.

Sunday morning. Hong Kong - Beijing on Dragonair. Yes, they were actually planning to take off into this typhoon! Now it's one thing to decide to land in a typhoon when you've flown in from the other side of the planet, are low on fuel and are reasonably keen to be somewhere on the ground. It seems to me quite another matter when you're already sitting safe and sound earthbound, and decide, for the hell of it, to leap voluntarily into the eye of a tropical storm.

Remember we mere passengers thought it was just raining out there, and had believed the old parking-at-the-hangar yarn. So, along with all the others, I was surprised when they issued us each at the departure gate with a see-through plastic mac. Anyway, we obediently pulled them on and stood around for 15 minutes looking a bit like Woody Allen's team of sperm particles, ready for whatever action may come their way. We bundled onto the bus without any problem; it was getting from the bus into the plane where the action was. When the bus pulled up at the foot of the steps to the plane, those nearest the door clattered out into the rain and scurried up the steps. Within 30 seconds most of them were back on the bus. It turned out the rain was horizontal and powered by a gale force wind, so that if you stood around in a queue on the steps for more than two seconds, you, your hand luggage, your clothes and your pac-a-mac turned into instant dishwater. So, resourceful and flexible as we passengers are, we developed a system. One person (he was English[52] but it wasn't me) stood as near the door as he dare and peered through the storm to the top of the steps. When he saw no-one blocking the door, he'd shout "Go!", and whoever thought they were next made a dash for the steps, scuttled up at a crouch to keep their head from being torn off by the wind and made a dive for the

---

[52] We may wear silly hats, but we're better at crises than the Chinese.

169

safety of the cabin. Then the next: "Go!", scuttle, crouch, dive. "Go!", scuttle, crouch, dive. I was now psychologically prepared for a parachute jump and if they were to extend the Olympic triple jump to the Triple Scuttle, I'd be in there with a chance of Gold for Britain.

As we waited for take-off, I wondered about the physical properties of a thousand tonnes of metal in a horizontal airflow at low pressure and wished, not for the first time, that I'd paid more attention at LEGS in Scruff's O-level Physics classes, instead of trying to turn the pulleys into catapults with Ian Hopkins. The pilot (again, reassuringly British – or maybe Chinese with elocution lessons) came on the intercom to tell us there was "a bit of weather out there", but that he was confident there'd be less of it about "upstairs". Obviously a highly trained meteorologist. Actually he was right: after a bumpy take-off, we did soon emerge into a sunlit paradise above the clouds that must have been there all the time.

Sunday lunchtime. Beijing International Airport. No dodgy landing, but no luggage either. Dragonair had managed the feat of being the first airline ever, after 35 years of flying, to lose my bags. I was directed to the Lost Luggage Office, which turned out to be the stage set from *Till Death Us Do Part*, i.e. Alf Garnett's living room: a few beaten-up armchairs, a few ashtrays, and lots of unwashed coffee cups lying around. No luggage, but plenty of forms and various people filling them in on the arms of the armchairs. A young and harassed Chinese woman asked me the redundant question: "Rost ruggage?", and showed me how to fill in the form. This was the start of a long and tedious procedure first to find my 'ruggage' and then to get some compensation for its late arrival – a procedure which was finally concluded some three months later… and of which, you'll be relieved to know, I'll spare you the gory, blow-by-blow account. Suffice it to say that this, and not the adventure with Typhoon Dot, is why Dragonair filled the bottom slot in my newly compiled World Airline Ratings, with 1 point. (To get 0 points you actually have to kill me in flight.)

Snee Goo Bee

Sunday afternoon. I should point out the timing of this trip. Two days earlier the city to host the 2000 Olympics had been chosen, and it was not, after all, Beijing. I wasn't sure whether someone coming from Barcelona, the most recent hosts, would be welcome or not. All over the airport, and indeed all over the city, no-one had yet got around to taking down the signs that proclaimed, in English, "A More Open China Awaits the 2000 Olympics". Maybe their slogan-writers just didn't show enough panache. Atlanta had probably secured the 1996 Games with something like "Let's Sock It To Socrates and Give Us The Big OG!"

Despite my apprehension, people could not have been friendlier. Not many spoke much English, but their enthusiasm to try and their keenness to help was everywhere and seemingly limitless. My taxi-driver welcomed me: "Wecom to Pekin", and gave me a hot flannel to help me freshen up[53].

So there was another surprise. Having assumed that "Beijing" was somehow politically correct, I now discovered that no-one had told the Chinese, who still called it "Peking". At least they did when they spoke English. Goodness knows what they really called it.

"Where you flom?"

"I'm English but I live in Spain."

"Fus tam in Pekin?"

"Yes, it's my first time in China." (Getting chatty now.) "I say, it's a pity about the Olympics ... I'm sorry Peking didn't get it."

Silence.

"I mean I think it would have been good for China to host the Olympics, don't you?"

"Solly, no speak Ingrish."

So his first three sentences had been learned parrot-fashion! But at least he spoke more English (some) than I did Chinese (zero), and *I* was in *his* country. After about two minutes, he said:

"Snee goo bee."

"I'm sorry?"

---

[53]I've since figured out that it's the hot flannel that turns a taxi into a limousine – that and the driver's white gloves. Oh, and the most important distinction: limousines already know what hotel you're staying at, indeed they work there and so you can add the fare to your room bill. I'm explaining this because it had been a complete mystery to me ever since I saw the signs to both "taxis" and "limos" in American airports. Of course, it's a complete con and highly elitist, but after the nightmare with Dragonair, I was not too reluctant to be molly-coddled.

"Snee! Vel goo bee!"

I got it: Sydney – a very good bid! Brilliant! Not only had the driver worked hard to figure out my comment in English, but he also chose the right thing to say. I was impressed.

Beijing's airport was on the east of the city and so was my hotel. So the taxi – sorry limo – ride was an uninspiring cruise along a dual carriageway that could have been anywhere in the world, with two exceptions. First, there was hardly any traffic. And second, the toll booth for this stretch of motorway was a spectacular red and gold pagoda that stood out from the grey skies and the grey environment like – well, like a pagoda on a motorway.

The Importance of the Inside Leg

We pulled up at the China World Hotel[54], one of the big grey blocks on Jianquomendajie Road (literally Road of the Big Grey Blocks). One of the doormen leapt to the boot of the limo, only to be disappointed at finding just a shoulder bag and a mysterious poster tube... you'll recall the rest of my luggage was somewhere between Barcelona, Zurich and Hong Kong. Nevertheless he carried his small quarry with panache through to the reception desk for me. Now, normally, I can't stand being waited on hand and foot like this – partly because, like many Brits, I'm a terrible tipper in the sense that I've never got the hang of how to do it without embarrassment, and partly because I object to having a service foisted on me without any choice in the matter. But the guidebooks said tipping is not the done thing in China, and everywhere porters, taxi-drivers, waiters and so on seemed to take such pleasure in serving you and, when the job was done, disappeared with such alacrity that it would have actually required some physical intervention to try and offer a tip. So I happily accepted all the service free. (The following day, however, I broke this rule when a driver had given service way beyond the call of duty and I gave him two US dollars. He seemed stunned. I hoped it wasn't because he was insulted by a tip, but rather because it was something approaching a day's wage.)

---

[54]Its name was in English and nothing else... there were no Chinese characters next to the English. I can only assume that if you couldn't read English, you couldn't afford to stay there.

172

I checked in and was escorted, bag, tube and all, to my room on the ninth floor. Now, there were three things I was dying to do: explore the facilities of what was clearly the most luxurious hotel I'd ever stayed in; escape from this ludicrous luxury and wander around in Beijing (hardly believing I was here); and fall into bed after a sleepless 30-hour journey. And the tedious truth was, of course, that I couldn't do any of these until I'd bought some clothes.

What a chore! I had actually changed once en route – all who have endured long-distance flights will know what a boost it is to be able to change your socks mid-flight. But now even the second set of clothes was getting pretty high[55] and anyway, I was due to make a presentation to some computer dealers the next day, and needless to say my suit and other presentable clothes were currently somewhere over (rather than *in*, I trusted) the Gobi Desert. So it was shop or die. If there's one activity I hate more than shopping, it's shopping for clothes in a foreign country of whose language I know not a word and whose prices are displayed in a different currency from the one I'm issued with. Chinese currency was the Yuan. But foreigners were not trusted with these: instead, we were issued with something called Foreign Exchange Certificates (FECs). I never did figure out the exchange rate between the two, nor the rate between either and the dollar (I was rightly advised by a colleague at work to bring U.S. dollars, as neither pesetas nor pounds would have cut much ice over here).

Now you might think that, to buy clothes in Beijing, I'd have to venture down some side street into some dark opium den of a tailors. Some people might even regard that as an enriching experience, but, when it comes to clothes, being a chap, I want it quick, simple and most certainly unenriching. (Six months earlier I'd travelled from Barcelona to Gibraltar to get my jeans from a Marks and Spencer's). For once my luck was in. The concierge told me there was a shopping complex in the very same building as the hotel, meaning it might even be aimed at foreigners. I dived down the escalator he indicated and emerged in what could have been Nottingham's Broadmarsh Shopping Centre, except that all the shops were about the size of tobacconists. I spotted two clothes shops and made a quick reckie of the racks. I was staring intently at the labels (searching for any recognizable clue to the size... a problem I hadn't

---

[55] Having just come down from 33,000 feet.

173

overcome in Spain either), when a young woman sneaked up on me and said something Chinese in my ear.

"Xuanliandonglu?"

I figured that, in a shop full of Chinese persons, it's unlikely that someone would ask directions of the single round-eyed demon, and therefore deduced that she was an assistant and wanted to know if she could help me.

"Ah, I'm looking for some trousers – do you speak English?"

"Ingrish. Rittle rittle."

"Er, Français? Deutsch?"

Blank. This showed I really was straight off the plane. Whatever the Académie Française or the Goethe Institute might hope, it should be obvious after only an hour of arrival that English is the *only* non-Asian language in China. And *faux pas* number two: "Rittle rittle" is Chinglish for "Well, I'm not exactly fluent, but I speak a damn sight more of your language than you do of mine. Shoot."

"Er, OK, English. My problem, as you can see, is that I'm short and fat, and so I'm looking for some trousers with short legs."

"You wan shots?"

"No, no, not shorts – trousers, but with short legs compared to the waist." I accompanied this with some graphic hand movements that were supposed to indicate the importance of the inside leg measurement, but which succeeded only in drawing a small crowd.

After some rolling of her eyes, the assistant said, "Major. I Major".

Either it was the Prime Minister in drag or she was going to measure me.

The crowd stayed put while she went for the tape major. Some children were giggling, so I busied myself re-inspecting the labels until my saviour eventually returned and started taking measurements. While she measured my inside leg (and while I hoped it wasn't too obvious that I'd worn these jeans from the Himalayas to Beijing via Hong Kong), I played to the crowd by patting my oversize stomach and raising an eyebrow, a little routine that the children thought this was hilarious. I was wondering if I could make a living in China as a clown when the assistant gave me the bad news:

"Impossiboo."

This was no surprise. I explained that I'd have to have them shortened.

"No plobrem. Leady tomollow dis time."

Tomollow dis time would be no good for me, so I picked a pair of trousers and gesticulated that I'd shorten them myself somehow... at least that was the intention of the series of gestures at my watch, my ankles and then my chest. She was a trifle confused, but when I opened my wallet and said "I buy them ... I pay now?", she soon got the message.

While she was wrapping them up, and while the crowd dispersed after their free entertainment, I rummaged through some shirts. Another assistant quickly sprung to my aid. (They could use some of these Chinese assistants in Spanish shops, where you'd have to drop your pants before you warrant precedence over the two prime activities of most shop assistants there: gossiping and smoking.)

"Ah, do you have any shirts with other kinds of buttons?"

"Bottons? No rike bottons?"

"Well, they're all golden. Do you have any shirts with, say, white buttons?"

Confusion, and then she said: "All bottons same. I think you rike this one." And she waved one of the shirts at me.

Well done, the sales training was good. I actually knew my neck measurement (I don't know why I can remember that and forget all the others... but at least when they hang me, presumably for serial sarcasm, there'll be no awkward delay while they find the right noose). She translated the size and added the shirt, plus a tie she'd chosen for me, to the trousers. They rang up my bill. The numbers meant nothing much to me, so I offered them some FECs and they soon figured it out.

Mission accomplished.

Street Life

Sunday evening. A colleague from Singapore was staying in the same hotel and I'd arranged to meet him for dinner at eight. This gave me just enough time for a quick scout around the neighbourhood before it got dark.

I walked down the long curving taxi ramp to the street. Escape from the protection of the hotel and into Beijing! I was actually walking in Peking'' Jianguomendajie Road is the main east-west axis across the centre of Beijing. About three miles west of the China World Hotel it crosses Tiananmen Square, between the Gate of Heavenly Peace, where Mao's portrait looks down over the square, and the Monument to the People's Heroes. I hoped to visit the square the next day, but didn't expect the People's Heroes to include those killed there four years before. It was strange to see signs pointing to a place whose name is so evocative to foreigners, but I suppose it's the same sensation for visitors to London when they see that there's a tube station called Baker Street.

Jianguomendajie Road is a dual carriageway and, as I emerged from the hotel, the traffic noise was intense. Ting! Ting ting!! Tingalingaling!!! Traffic in China means bicycles. Hundreds of them, thousands of them, everywhere you go: the standard and classless form of transport. There were men in overalls on bikes, women in skirts on bikes, children on bikes, youths on bikes, grandmothers on bikes, grizzled old men on bikes, soldiers on bikes; bikes pulling rickshaws, bikes pulling empty trailers, bikes pulling other bikes, bikes pulling carts with all manner of merchandise – bags of flour, bales of straw, drums of oil, cages of live chickens, unidentifiable white bags, unidentifiable black blobs. Millions of bikes. It was overwhelming and I loved it. In every city in the world, cities without hills that is, private cars and motorcycles should be banned. Why not?

The only motor vehicles on Jianguomendajie Road were taxis and buses – old 1950s-style buses, like Barton's X99 from Nottingham to Birmingham, but packed to and beyond the gunnels with passengers. I didn't see or hear a single motor bike or moped all the time I was in China, and after four years on the moped-infested European Continent, this came as a breath of fresh air.

I walked a couple of blocks westward and then tried to cross the main road. I chose the only crossing I'd seen where there were traffic lights, though there was also a white-uniformed policeman standing, waving and whistling, on a round white block in the middle of the junction. I don't know whether he was having any effect, because however he waved and whatever the lights did, there was always a stream of traffic coming from one direction or another on every square inch of road. And yet people were crossing. I decided to stand and observe these pedestrians for a while to see how they did it.

How to Cross the Street in a Chinese City Without Being Bicycled to Death

1. Wander nonchalantly off the kerb, always facing upstream in terms of the bike flow.
2. Stop only when the nearest bikes are brushing past your nose.
3. Look upstream and identify a gap that will soon pass you (a gap is anything greater than half a bike's length).
4. Fix the rider of the bike behind the gap with a defiant stare.
5. When the gap arrives, saunter nonchalantly across the street, still outstaring the chosen cyclist.

With this method, the other hundred or so cyclists hurtling in from behind should pick up your body language and swerve to avoid you. *Should.* I implemented this plan and did manage to get to the other side of the street more or less unscathed, but my nonchalance may have been a little hard to spot, given that I was skipping around like a matador without a cape.

I turned left down Menbeidajie Road. (If you're wondering how I know these street names, it's because, fortunately for us round-eyed demons, the street signs for the main roads in Beijing are written both in Mandarin and Romanized characters. So although you may not know what it means nor how to say it, at least you can compare it with a name on a street map.) This took me into a network of alleys that could have been transplanted from nineteenth-century Manchester. It took me a while to realize that the little huts and sheds with the fires outside and the children playing in the doorways were actually houses. The ones with electric light bulbs were shops and the ones with the chairs outside were bars. It was poor all right, but no-one seemed hungry, there were no beggars, and I realized after turning a few corners that what made it definitely non-European was that there was hardly any litter and no graffiti at all.

Of course everyone stared at me. Men in bars stopped with their beer halfway to their lips. Children stood aghast. Some youths kicking stones around at a corner plucked up the courage to shout "Harro!" I waved and called back "Hallo, how are you!" This seemed to be the best joke they'd heard all day, strengthening my conviction that I could profitably swap computers for comedy out

177

here. However, it was dark now, getting cold and beginning to drizzle. I didn't have my coat (it being somewhere over, or possibly in, the Ganges delta), and so I made my way back to the main road and to the hotel.

News of Fresh Disasters

My hotel room was approximately the size of Belgium and the bed could probably have housed half its population. The contents of my hand luggage didn't really do the wardrobe justice. I changed into the complimentary bathrobe, put on the complimentary slippers and switched on the TV, which I was then able to listen to in the shower, since there were speakers everywhere. The news was about Typhoon Dot in the South China Sea and the havoc it had caused, something I knew about first hand. Then, as I was drying my hair, David Frost interviewed Terry Waite. I mention this because, during the same time that Mr Waite had been hostage in Beirut, I'd been voluntarily hostage in France and Spain and therefore listening to the BBC News was a rare treat, which I was to enjoy every evening of my stay in the East. I'd never heard Terry Waite's voice before. This was rather less of a shock than the time, a few months earlier, when I first heard John Major's voice. In his case, I think the continental dubbed versions were an improvement.

The phone rang and it was Victor from Singapore, but currently in Room 937.

"I'm hungry – why not eat right now?", he said.

"OK."

"I'll meet you in the Japanese restaurant on the third floor in five minutes. I'll be wearing a yellow sweater." (We'd never met before.)

"OK. Five minutes. I'm short and dumpy with glasses and a moustache."

He laughed. "Don't worry, Richard, I'll recognize you."

Of course – spotting an Englishman in a Japanese restaurant in Beijing is a doddle. Suddenly I remembered I'd done nothing about my trousers. Darn! Or rather, safety pins! On the off chance, I pulled open a few drawers and found I was in luck again – there, complete with pins of all shapes and sizes, was a miniature sewing kit – for the visitor in sartorial distress. That was me all right. What a hotel! A quick fold-and-pin job, and I was shuffling down to the third floor in pair of trousers with six-inch internal turn-ups, and a gold-buttoned shirt. And they say Englishmen don't know how to dress!

Well, after I'd regaled Victor over the sushi with details of my incident-packed journey, he brought news of fresh disasters. Not only would I have no suit for the presentation and no slides (somewhere over the Mekong Delta), but neither would I have a product to demonstrate, as there'd been some hold-up in customs. Oh well, this may make the day's work even shorter and therefore mean more time to explore the Mysterious East! Evly crowd has a sivver rining!

After the meal, we went down to the bar for a beer. Even with my gold buttons I felt a little underdressed for the lounge bar of the China World Hotel. It extended to the height of two floors and the decorated ceiling was supported on eight ornate columns. At one end of the lounge a string quartet was playing. While all the waiters in the restaurant had been men, here there were only waitresses. Well, the waiters would have looked a little odd in the split skirts that seemed to be the standard uniform in Chinese hotel bars wherever I went. When I asked Victor why his English was so good, he told me about being at university in New Zealand, where his fellow students seemed to care about nothing but rugby and women. This sounded much like being at university in Wales, I commented; but this potentially interesting line of discussion had to await another time as I was dropping off to sleep as we spoke, and so we arranged to meet for breakfast and retired.

About 34 hours after waking up in a tiny flat in Barcelona, I eventually climbed into an emperor-sized bed in Beijing, and immediately fell into the sleep of the just knackered.

The Mysteries of the Occident

You don't have to travel to the Far East, however, to encounter a land of mystery where misunderstanding reigns supreme. The Rongest Day had been preceded by other, less exotic business trips, and here are two short tales from the Near West…

My first trip to the island of Ireland took me to Belfast in the middle of the Troubles[56]. When I approached my hotel, therefore, all I saw was barricades, boarded-up windows and a heavily bolted door, to the side of which was a very small light with a very small button. I pressed the very small button and through a very small speaker spoke a very small voice.

"Whoy az it?"

"Erm, I'm a guest of the hotel."

A few seconds of silence, and then:

"Come an, guest."

The door unbolted and then opened. I entered a rather dim reception area, where a very small man sat behind a very small desk. After the formalities, he allocated me Room 93 and handed me the key, which was marked '72'.

"Er, I think this is the wrong key – you said Room 93."

"That is the key to Room 93."

"But…"

"They're all marked '72'." And to prove it, he waved at the key rack behind him, where about twenty keys hung, all indeed marked '72'.

"Um, why is that exactly?"

He eyed me suspiciously, glanced either side and then gestured me towards him.

"Security!", he whispered.

My second trip to Ireland gave me a free weekend sandwiched between two meetings and I took the opportunity to escape to the west; to Galway in fact, which had always sounded an attractive, windy, fishy, Atlantic sort of a place.

The train was packed and I sat opposite a tall, tweeded and talkative gentleman. In fact, the most obvious difference between a British and an Irish train is that in Ireland the passengers talk to each other. My companion opened up soon after departure.

"So where are you off, sur?"

"I'm going to Galway. And you?"

---

[56] Is there anywhere but the middle?

"Ah, Gaalwee. Yes, I'm away there too."

A few seconds silence and he resumed:

"You don't have a care!"

"Erm, I'm sorry?"

"You're on the train, so you don't have a care."

"Ah, no, I absolutely agree – it's the best way to travel."

At this point, I noticed the hubbub had died a little and the other passengers had zeroed into our conversation.

"I do," continued the tweedy one.

"Oh really, I'm sorry. What's the problem?"

"No problem at all – it's an escort."

(Sniggers from other seats.)

"Ah, I think you've lost me – why do you have cares? Is he a bad escort?"

"It's a Ford Escort!"

"Oh, a car!!"

At which, to a man, the rest of the carriage burst into laughter and the boy next to me couldn't help mimicking my English accent:

"Oh, a cah!!"

17. Alas, it would have to wait a few more years yet. Promotional poster for the Olympic bid that was pipped at the post by Sydney. Beijing, October, 1993. *Photo: author*.

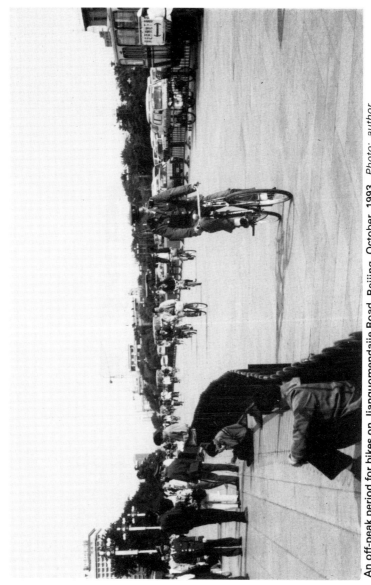

18. An off-peak period for bikes on Jianquomendajie Road, Beijing October, 1993. *Photo: author*

183

19. Come in, Number 4!   Time is up for one dignitary on Tiananmen
Square. Beijing, October, 1993.   *Photo: author*

9

Grounded

All good things come to an end, and the better they are, the swifter they seem to end. A good curry at the Amirul in Quorn should last a couple of hours, but the best meal on Earth – a bag of fish and chips from Tennant's on Station Road, Long Eaton – will be over inside fifteen minutes. And then the most delicious individual item of food possible – a chocolate-covered Merry Maid caramel, purchased from the Conway Street confectioner's now sadly disappeared – used to be gone inside two minutes[57]. Ho hum.

My seven years abroad were over way too soon. Despite all my whingeing, all the incomprehensible paperwork, all the misunderstandings – and especially all the ghastly food, which I haven't even told you about... despite all this, every morning on the Continent I awoke feeling more alive than I'd ever felt in England. Some folks are happiest surrounded by the familiar, by friends and family in a place where they're settled, but I'm evidently one of those at the other end of the spectrum: familiarity breeds unease, so that I'm constantly yearning to get on to the next place, where another unknown environment will give its positive charge to my cells. In the early '80s I flew to Australia alone and the memory of that first hour walking across Sydney, completely anonymous in an alien city on the other side of the planet, still brings a zing to my soul.

But in 1996 family affairs called me back to England, as I knew all along that they would. I was grounded, and being grounded in a terraced house on Wellington Street, Long Eaton, is about as grounded as you can get.

---

[57] Nowadays, of course, a caramel lasts a lot longer since I'm allowed only to suck it, lest its chewing detaches half my dental repairs.

While physically Long Eaton itself had hardly changed, except for the traffic and the Co-op clock being in even worse states than when I'd left, England and its people had moved on. I'm not sure I liked where they'd moved on to.

Surely people didn't used to be as ugly as this! After France and Spain, humans over here looked like a different species: mostly fat, badly dressed, too often with hideously dyed hair and, unbelievably, with pins and studs stuck to the most gruesome parts of their visible anatomy. Had an alien craft, crewed only by drug-crazed punks and bad hairdressers, landed while I was away and replaced the gentlefolk that used to inhabit these islands? And were those baseball caps with their extravagantly curved peaks part of the alien uniform?

Such strange behaviour too! Fear and hatred for all things foreign, race riots, children leaping up and down like mad dogs, door-to-door threats on Hallowe'en, burning cars on back lanes... this looked very much like the end of empire to me. And no longer was there an escape to a more civilized world through television, for there the lunatics seemed to have taken over the asylum. The screen in the corner, which used to bring such geniuses as Hancock, Morecambe, Cleese and Atkinson[58] into the living room, was dominated by either an annoying, ginger-topped madman called Evans or a whining, Brummie simpleton called Tarrant, who I thought had reached his intellectual level in *Tiswas* – and I was right. These grinning goons presented 'shows' in which countless, talent-free nonentities were wheeled onto the stage to be greeted by the sort of manic cheering and whooping that might be reserved for a second coming of the Messiah.

Life back in the English-speaking empire did have its compensations though. Just being able to phone a plumber with a passably coherent description of my latest toiletry problem was invaluable. And I hadn't previously appreciated the value of such incredibly widespread and generously subsidized evening classes: what a boon they are to witless and ignorant yokels like me! History, Spanish, politics, guitar-playing, drawing, astronomy... you name it, I imbibed it.

---

[58] Rowan, not Ron.

Ten Unfathomable Mysteries

All this late education, however, has not – even to this day – helped me solve the following unfathomable mysteries that confronted me on my arrival back in late-20th-century England.

1. When and why was the word for the biological distinction between male and female ('sex') replaced by the word for the grammatical distinction between masculine and feminine ('gender')?

2. Why have people on fair rides suddenly started waving their arms in the air like deranged Italian traffic policemen?

3. When did news journalists stop reporting the news (i.e. what has happened – past tense) and start predicting the future? "This morning, the home secretary *will* announce... later today, a wide-ranging report *will* recommend... tomorrow a small meteorite *will* hit Broadcasting House." No, that last one was just wishful thinking.

4. Where did the blue skies and white hills of winter go?

5. What catastrophe transformed my former heroes and European champions, Nottingham Forest, into a panic-stricken bunch of has-beens and never-will-bes who couldn't dribble a football past a stationary gravestone?

6. Why can't teenagers tie their shoelaces?

7. What intonational force has pulled the stress from the back to the front of a whole raft of everyday words now enunciated as *ice*-cream, *re*search, *cig*arette, *mag*azine etc etc?

8. When did 'films' become 'movies'? (And when did they stop showing them at the 'pictures'?)

9. Why did the local 'railway station' become the 'train station'?

10. And most mysteriously of all, did the English language's entire genitive case accidentally fall down a well, or get lost somewhere else in the seven years I was away? What had been Curry's has become Currys; the Turk's Head has become the Turks Head (where do they head?); and, perversely, the 1960s has become the 1960's. Yes, the country's entire stock of apostrophes had apparently been thrown into the air like so much confetti, to fall randomly in quite inappropriate places. Did someone at the Department of Education spill the Tippex

over a certain page of the third-year English curriculum? I think we deserve to know!

I suspect the answer to many of these questions, my friend, is blowin' in the wind that carries Americans and their 'culture' across the Atlantic. The Big O's "wop-wop-woo"s and The Cisco Kid's hat are one thing (well, all right, two); but the inanity of Ruby Wax and South Park are quite another.

The eleventh mystery, of course, is how I'd suddenly become so middle-aged. One Friday in July 1996, I'd jumped into Sutty (for he still served me well) with all my belongings and set off from Spain, still a relatively bright and youthful fortysomething. Three days later I fetched in Wellington Street a grumpy old git.

Livid of Long Eaton

Finding myself once again in a country where newsprint appeared in my native language, I began to let off steam via that wonderful free institution, the Letter to the Editor. Me and hundreds of other grumpy old gits. I understand the Letters column doesn't exist in some newspapers abroad; certainly I don't recall seeing any in the odd 'paper I struggled through in French, Spanish or Catalan. What a rich source of entertainment they're missing, not to mention the savings to the health services afforded by these self-therapeutic columns.

In one of the newspapers that's published some letters of mine, they include your full address, and so I've had the extra fun of receiving personal mail from a whole string of patriotic, right-wing, royalist lunatics – a startling number of whom write in purple ink and stick little union jacks on the backs of their envelopes. I can't tell you how much pleasure I get from despatching them all very quickly into the bin, where the photos of various monarchs and prime ministers that they often enclose can find their natural home among the worms and snails of my refuse.

Locally, I began inflicting monthly tirades on *The Long Eaton Advertiser* and then, after moving house, redirected my fire to *The Loughborough Echo*. These two venerable institutions both contain within their Letters pages an incomparable array of local characters, whose preoccupations bear little relation to the vital issues of 21st-century Plant Earth   and which are the more fascinating for that.

The Advertiser boasts the prolific S T Wood, whose sole mission in life is to have Erewash Borough Council remove the weeds from the uncared-for pavements of his beloved Sandiacre. Another regular contributor is David Tobias, whose specialist subject, indeed only subject, is The Villainy of the Windsor Family and whose letters, I feel, are all written not in ink but in the blood of the proletariat.

The Echo's pages are fuller and include the sort of well-constructed and incisive letters you'd expect from a university town. However, easily the most controversial views have come from the 'Reverend' Leslie Robinson, although who it is that revered him was never revealed. 'Robbo' is a muscular Christian, whose views on life and its distasteful current representatives are untainted by such irrelevant distractions as truth or reason... or even knowledge. The only words of value are the Words of God, right or wrong. I'm proud to say that Robbo has personally condemned me to 'the lake of fire' for my view of Christianity (viz. that it's all codswallop), and I've promised him that, should I, shortly after death, find myself perched on a ledge above the said lake, I'll do my best to send him a postcard admitting my error.

Given that I haven't exactly been hiding my desk lamp under a bushel, it's ironic that the Inland Revenue refused to admit I exist.

An Existential Tale (or Two)

When I left Spain, I only half-existed. Administratively, that is. Due to a certain sequence of events with which I shall not burden you, but which involved a non-residential resident's permit, an unidentifiable identity card and the Maastricht Treaty[59], I returned to these shores with an uncertain status, but confident of course that HMG would swiftly restore me to normality. And then I contacted the dear old Inland Revenue.

I wasn't especially over-eager to resume paying British taxes, but the fact that a significant Spanish customer (for whom I was by now working on a freelance basis) would withhold 25% of what they owed me unless I could prove I was paying my British taxes, rather pushed me in that direction.

---

[59] ... and which, if you really want your brain numbed by it, appears in *Sutty's Tale* (the book) as "An Existential Tale".

I duly phoned my old 'Nottingham 2' tax office with the good news that I was back.

"Long Eaton, sir? You're now under 'Derby 1'."

I phoned Derby 1.

"You're not on our files, sir."

"I just got back from Spain."

"Ah, you'll be under Bootle."

"As in Merseyside?"

"Yes."

"Like to tell me why?"

"Bootle deals with non-residents."

"But I'm resident now."

"They'll decide that, sir."

"Er, Bootle 1, is it?"

"Bootle 6278."

I phoned Bootle 6278.

"Revenue!"

I explained my business.

"You want 7098."

I phoned Bootle 7098.

"Revenue!"

I explained my business.

"You want 6278. No, I'm sorry, sir, you do."

(El Rack all over again .)

I phoned Bootle 6278.

"Ah yes, you're disputing your residence status, are you, sir?"

"Well, I'm resident here; if anyone's disputing it, that would be you."

"Ah, I see. Just a moment, sir."

There followed a few grunts, some thuds, as of large cardboard boxes being shifted, some rather echoey steps, the rustle of paper, more steps and then Mr 6278 again.

"Um, this may take some time, sir. I'll fax you."

I can't help imagining that the thudding boxes contained details of the thousands of cases where people were arguing with the Inland Revenue that they were *not* in fact UK-resident and would *not* in fact be paying their taxes. The box containing just my own little file, where I argued quite the opposite, expressing my veritable keenness to pay my taxes, must have been so small as to have temporarily disappeared. This was confirmed by Mr 6278's fax: "I would confirm that I am currently trying to trace your file. You will be duly advised on progress."

Well, 'duly' slipped into 'overduly' and 18 weeks (*eighteen weeks!*) after my accountant had formally asked Bootle to confirm my residency status – and a whopping 48 weeks (*forty-eight weeks!*) after I'd initially offered to pay the Inland Revenue my dues – he was able to write to me: "I am pleased to say that at last the Revenue has retrieved your file from the bottom of the Mersey."

The breakthrough seems to have been my letter on the subject to my MP, who passed it to my MEP, who passed it to the Chairman of the Board of the Inland Revenue, Sir Anthony Battishall. Sir Ant received my letter of complaint on July 18th; I received a fax from Bootle stating that I was indeed a UK tax resident on, er, July 18th. I don't know what Sir Ant had said to Mr 6278, but the fax included a strange little box below the contact details stating in bold letters: "HELP ME". (I am not making this up.)

I wonder if a besuited body appeared at the bottom of the Mersey to mark the spot where my file had been found?

So in the end, I have to admit that the Poncets of France and the Jesters of Spain were not, after all, so unusual in the brave new world of the EU – in terms of sheer bureaucratic intransigence, the Bootles of England leave them streets, *boulevards* and whole *avenidas* behind.

The Long-Running Affair: Epilogue

So, though temporarily grounded, I'm keeping my spirits up by continuing to distribute regular dollops of sarcasm in all directions – a life-giving therapy I'd recommend to anyone. Although I've wangled an early retirement from my long-running professional affair with the computer, it still seems to be keeping an eye on me from the corner of the room. After I'd been hovering indecisively over a web page for a few minutes, the following message just appeared:

You've been idle for too long.

Other Books by Richard Guise:

Moments in Time (with others) (1996)
The Limerick Gazetteer of Great Britain (1998)
Breaking Cover (with others) (2001)
Neddytown: A History of Draycott and Church Wilne (2001)

All are available from the author at:

richard_guise@yahoo.com